Valuing Diversity: The Primary Years

Janet Brown McCracken

A 1992–93 NAEYC Comprehensive Membership benefit

NATIONAL ASSOCIATION FOR THE EDUCATION
OF YOUNG CHILDREN
WASHINGTON, DC

In our every deliberation,
we must consider the impact of our decisions
on the next seven generations.

—The Great Law of the Six Nations
of the Iroquois Confederacy

Weaving on cover: Sally Bachman; *Cover design:* Polly Greenberg and Jack Zibulsky

Photographs: pp. vi, 20, 57, 64, 74—© Subjects & Predicates; p. 5—© Marilyn Nolt; p. 9—© Barbara Brockmann; pp. 15, 28, 35, 88—© BmPorter/Don Franklin; p. 41—© Jeffrey High Image Productions; p. 51—© Lillis Larson-Kent; p. 82—© Harvey R. Phillips/PPI.

National Association for the Education of Young Children (NAEYC)
1509 16th Street, N.W.
Washington, DC 20036–1426

The National Association for the Education of Young Children attempts through its publications program to provide a forum for discussion of major issues and ideas in our field. We hope to provoke thought and promote professional growth. The views expressed or implied are not necessarily those of the Association. NAEYC wishes to thank the author, who donated much time and effort to develop this book as a contribution to our profession.

ISBN #: 0–935989–55–2

Library of Congress #: 93–084576

NAEYC order #: 238

Editor: Polly Greenberg; *Production:* Jack Zibulsky and Penny Atkins; *Copyeditors:* Millie Riley and Betty Nylund Barr; *Editorial assistance:* Julie L. Andrews.

Printed in the United States of America

Contents

Why Value Diversity?

Why do caring people—children and adults—value human diversity? Each of us has our own reasons, notes Enid Lee, one of many impassioned voices speaking out on behalf of harmony among people.

Some of us value human uniqueness because it's the right thing to do. Respect for each other's heritages, personhood, and beliefs is an ethical commitment. We advocate for fairness, we promote compassion, and we stand up against prejudice and bias on principle. We strive to reach consensus, to get along with each other, to bring out the best in ourselves and others. Each new challenge strengthens our resolve to cherish human dignity.

People may also value diversity for pragmatic reasons. Some reason that if we appreciate each other, the world will surely become a more harmonious place in which to live and work. On the other hand, the results of perpetrating hate permeate history—and splash across today's newspapers. In our schools, duck-and-play-dead drills are becoming to the 1990s what civil-defense drills were to the 1950s.

Other people may tolerate each other, at least initially, because laws firmly establish human rights and prohibit discrimination, although clearly not universally—or even within the United States—for all people. Legal guarantees of civil rights are one baseline for creating a more civilized society.

All of us are learning to value and find strength in each other's diversity—in how we live and how we teach. Even those of us who are firmly committed to equality must still humbly struggle to reconcile our own conflicts and failings. If we engage in this learning process with a curious, open spirit, we begin to see history and the future in a different light. We come to realize that the better we know each other, the more likely we are to appreciate each other.

Teachers and families are encouraged to creatively pursue and elaborate on the ideas that this book briefly explores. Resources for helping children learn to value diversity surround us. We urgently need to learn to respect each other. Our strength lies in our diversity. Together we can build a fair and more peaceful planet—one child, one group at a time.

A Child's Right to the Valuing of Diversity

During the International Year of the Child, NAEYC joined other child groups to advocate for public responsibility to assure children's basic rights. Mary Lane, then director of the Oakland, California, Parent Child Center, authored this statement, which was published widely, including the September 1984 issue of Young Children. *Her message speaks with pressing urgency for today's world.*

G reat cultural diversity still exists on our planet, even as modern technology pushes for more uniformity and as McDonald's and Coca Cola spread everywhere. In ecological terms, we accept the principle of diversity for plants and animals. We protect endangered species—too late sometimes—in most of the civilized world. But if humankind is to maintain itself, the valuing of diversity must increase in our own lives also.

Indeed, *we* may become an endangered species unless we begin early to help our children learn to value diversity. How? By recognizing the rationale for such a position and then organizing society to achieve this goal.

As our world becomes even smaller, communication can be almost instantaneous. Mobility characterizes families more than stability. People in this kind of world must have these three qualities to succeed: (1) the ability to cope with change; (2) an open, flexible personality that enjoys the *process* of change; and (3) the ability to assimilate changes into a satisfying personal lifestyle. Diversity is the touchstone for each of these three qualities.

A child who associates with children who speak other languages, who worship in other ways, who eat other foods, whose skin color differs from one's own, and whose behavior suggests different upbringing, learns about the basic similarities of all people everywhere and can understand and appreciate their fascinating differences. Such children have many points of reference when they meet people with other values and when they encounter new situations.

Many of humankind's great upheavals have been caused by the blindness of those in power to the aspirations of people with whom they disagreed. The value of an open, flexible personality is well established.

Closed, rigid individuals are prone to prejudice, biased to the extent that they wear blinders to anything that does not match their early perceptions. On the other hand, children who have learned that people of all races and cultures have high ambitions and feel strongly about the quality of life; that love, peace, and respect are universal concepts regardless of the language used to express them—such children have incorporated the basics of an open, flexible approach to life.

Survival itself may well depend on the right to experience diversity and then to assimilate change. To evaluate the validity of experience for oneself and one's lifestyle is the outcome of thoughtfully charting a life course, as opposed to swaying with the whims of the times.

We who speak out for children must ensure that the nation who "tightens its belt" does not choke its future. We must speak out for the rights of children—to be nourished, to play, to imagine, and to value diversity.

—*Mary Lane*

Part 1

Exploring Classroom Resources

Intellect annuls fate.

—Ralph Waldo Emerson

Young children are natural and eager learners—from the moment they're born. They pick up skills, ideas, and attitudes by observing each other, their family members, and their child care providers. Between the ages of two and five, children become keenly aware of differences in ethnicity, abilities, and gender. Most young children also learn from other people within their communities, such as police officers, librarians, and grocery store clerks. Television has undoubtedly made its contribution, too.

By the time they begin formal schooling, children have learned to speak and understand at least one language. They have their own opinions and interests. Their successes (or failures) largely determine how they feel about themselves. At the same time they are still gradually gaining control of their behavior. They welcome opportunities to make their own decisions and to take responsibility. When children enter school they are already experienced and adept learners, and they are on the threshold of being able to think in more logical, concrete ways.

Most children enter their classrooms with high expectations about what they will achieve in kindergarten and throughout their primary years. They've heard all about school from siblings and friends. "What will my teachers be like?" they wonder. "What will I learn?" "Who will be my friends?" Children themselves, their families, communities, and the entire country entrust schools to nurture youth in ways that will bode them well for the future.

Chapter **1**

What Are Children Learning?

W hat are families and educators teaching America's children—who, after all, will soon be the world's leaders, labor force, and voters? Frank Smith states it succinctly: "Students learn exactly what they are taught" (1986, p. ix).

As we choose themes, materials, and teaching strategies, we keep our ultimate goal in mind: we are preparing children to lead rewarding, productive lives in a peaceful world that always has been, and surely always will be, diverse. More specific educational goals for children are best phrased as questions:

• Are children learning to love their quest for knowledge?

• Are children learning to see themselves as competent communicators, inquirers, and discoverers?

• Are children learning to negotiate and collaborate in democratic ways?

• Are children learning to understand and appreciate our world's rich diversity of cultures, heritages, abilities, and interests?

• Are children learning to apply all of their knowledge to build strong futures for themselves and others?

Most primary-level program goals weave perfectly within this broad framework. The goals for Americans All (Table 1), one outstanding national education program, are derived from theories on multicultural development, motivation, self-esteem, and stress and learning (Christopher, 1990).

Children who are equipped with knowledge and appreciation of the splendid variety of people who live and work in the world will most likely be wise parents and productive workers. Those who comprehend the rocky road of human history—and the tribulations and triumphs that have come before the United States and other relatively new nations—will surely make astute decisions as they add their chapters to human history.

Teaching: Substance and *style*

These ambitious but realistic goals can be reached with and for children. Frank Smith continues his pointed remarks about American education by identifying the kind of teaching that leads to achievement of our goals:

> Sensitive and imaginative teachers inspire learning of lasting depth and complexity— a love of learning itself—in students with all kinds of interests and abilities. But success like this is achieved only when teacher and student have the mutual respect and trust that is the basis of all effective learning. (1986, p. x)

Groups of young children commonly celebrate a Mexican holiday with a piñata, make potato latkes as part of their winter festivities, try out a walker in the pretend play area, or read a story once a week with a retired volunteer. These activities may be carried out with the best of intentions and may even make children somewhat more aware of the world around them. Such tourist-type approaches, however, rarely broaden children's *genuine* under-

---

Educational goals for children

- Are children learning to love their quest for knowledge?
- Are children learning to see themselves as competent communicators, inquirers, and discoverers?
- Are children learning to negotiate and collaborate in democratic ways?
- Are children learning to understand and appreciate our world's rich diversity of cultures, heritages, abilities, and interests?
- Are children learning to apply all of their knowledge to build strong futures for themselves and others?

---

standing of themselves, their friends, and the other people with whom they will live near and work every day of their lives.

Hit-or-miss classroom activities on any topic are simply insufficient to establish a classroom permeated with success, trust, and mutual respect. Instead of relying on a few special activities to boost

---

Table 1. Americans All Program Goals

- Increased knowledge about self and the history and cultures of others
- Increased personal relevance of content and opportunities for self-expression
- Improved interpersonal and motivational skills
- Increased feelings of belonging and affiliation
- Increased opportunities for positive peer relationships and cross-cultural relationships
- Increased opportunities for success and validating feedback
- Improved stress management and coping skills
- Increased knowledge about self, family, community, and adaptation
- Improved student performance
- Decreased environmental stress
- Decreased student alienation and boredom

> # We are preparing children to lead rewarding, productive lives in a peaceful world that always has been, and surely always will be, diverse.

self-esteem or to highlight cultures and human diversity, in a truly success-oriented school, mutual respect and trust are embedded within *all* that children do during their day. Curriculum is what happens—the materials and the teaching strategies, the discipline and the projects, the languages spoken and written, the ways families are involved, the foods served for lunch, and the connections that are forged with the community.

Rather than demanding extra time and expensive equipment or materials, this *curriculum-is-what-happens* integrated approach to teaching heightens children's competence and self-esteem, makes the most of readily available human and material resources, empowers children to develop empathy and counteract bias, and reestablishes teaching as a lively, challenging profession. The ideas and materials suggested here are designed to be incorporated into the daily learning process and are based on the most reliable information available on how young children grow and learn.

Fostering children's intelligences

Every community, every school, every classroom contains a wealth of resources for learning. Even when budgets are mere shoestrings and supplies are limited, the primary instigators of learning always remain—children and their teachers.

Equipping a classroom with developmentally appropriate learning materials is just one small step in making it possible to amplify learning and facilitate relationships. People—children, families, teachers, administrators, and residents of the community—are the sparks who make learning come alive!

Recent research has revealed that people have at least seven different ways of knowing, or of processing information (Gardner, 1991). These seven intelligences wax and wane over our individual lifetimes, but each way of knowing is always present to some extent in all of us. In considering this list, consider how children and adults have strengths, and areas to be further developed, in all seven intelligences:

- linguistic (such as poets or writers),
- logical-mathematical (strongest in scientists or mathematicians),
- musical (performers or sophisticated listeners),
- spatial (perhaps artists or surgeons),
- bodily-kinesthetic (athletes or dancers are typical),
- interpersonal (getting along with others), and
- intrapersonal (self-knowledge).

The curriculum-is-what-happens *approach to teaching*

- heightens children's competence and self-esteem,
- makes the most of readily available resources,
- empowers children to develop empathy and counteract bias, and
- reestablishes teaching as a lively, challenging profession.

Our goals for children are far more likely to be reached if we view learning through this kaleidoscope of multiple ways of knowing; thus the ideas throughout this guide encourage teachers to encompass all of these human intelligences in planning for children and to capitalize on young children's intrinsic desire to learn.

The remainder of this first part of the book describes a unique, unfolding perspective on education that values human diversity. We start with a look at the commitments teachers must make to themselves and their communities. Guidelines are offered for selecting a wide variety of tangible resources that children, families, and educators have on hand or can easily assemble to create a classroom that embeds mutual trust and respect for all people. Ideas are also provided for preparing a well-rounded environment through learning materials, field trips,

Children's seven intelligences

- linguistic
- logical-mathematical
- musical
- spatial
- bodily-kinesthetic
- interpersonal
- intrapersonal

and guests, all of which are critical for keeping children in touch with and involved in the world around them.

Part 2 suggests ways to expand familiar teaching strategies and curriculum ideas with other appropriate resources to create a truly integrated approach to learning and teaching.

The third part of this brief guide lists selected children's books and identifies just enough resources to whet teachers' appetites for more professional-practice information.

The vision of flexible, enriching, integrated education can serve as a springboard from which children can celebrate their own—and our country's and world's—diversity.

In a truly success-oriented school, mutual respect and trust are embedded within all that children do.

Chapter 2

Liberating the Human Spirit

H anging above Carol Brunson Phillips's executive-suite desk is a plaque she earned at a spelling bee in the Chicago schools, a poignant reminder of her youthful achievements. Most of us treasure similar tokens—artwork from our childhood, notes teachers wrote to our parents, or photographs of our first bicycles—that remind us of how our early roots enabled us to flourish.

Phillips is an eminent and articulate early childhood educator who challenges all of us to grasp the realities of race and culture in society. As an advocate for children, their families, professionals, and the democratic principles upon which this country was founded, she identifies four ethical commitments for educators who strive to implement curricula that rest on trust and respect (Phillips, 1988, pp. 42–47).

Teachers are urged to challenge themselves to grow with these four commitments. Begin now to tackle the issues raised. Then, as experience with all areas of diversity accumulates, return again and again to these ethical statements. Why? In part because they provide a measure for professional progress; but most of all, these commitments establish direction for a life-long process that will enable us to stretch even further toward reaching the goals we share for all people.

COMMITMENT #1. Identify and examine how society—through its major institutions [such as] schools, health and welfare systems, government, and media—perpetuates racism and oppression in very obscure yet systematic ways.

Institutional racism in the United States cannot be denied, nor can it be ignored. By accepting that our society subtly, and sometimes blatantly, discriminates against and stereotypes people, we can better understand the realities of the lives of the children we teach. Only with this perception is it possible to establish a classroom atmosphere that values diversity. Nearly one third of U.S. students live in non-White, immigrant families (Ogbu, 1987), so a substantial portion of our population is affected by institutionalized barriers to success. By the year 2050 about one half of the U.S. population will be non–European, according to the Census Bureau.

Discussions, especially within diverse groups, are excellent ways to bring out differing experiences and perceptions of bias in society. Perhaps primary teachers in each building or school district could set aside staff-development time to begin to examine their own experiences, or teachers could arrange informal gatherings with parents in the community to gain a better understanding of their backgrounds. Reading, attending workshops, mulling over ideas with a friend or supervisor, or individual deliberations are other avenues to consider in starting the process of identifying systematic discrimination.

Whatever the route taken, each teacher can take an honest look at America's culture by detecting and analyzing patterns of discrimination. These are some questions that might be raised for discussion:

- Why are so many national and local leaders White males?

- What are the long-term implications of testing and tracking for children?

- Why are government budgets often balanced on the backs of people with the fewest resources?

- What kinds of role models are exemplified in sports? Movies? The news?

By assessing our society's strengths and weaknesses, teachers grow, both professionally and personally. As a result, teachers treat children more fairly and become better learning facilitators in their classrooms and communities. Kendall forthrightly acknowledges, "Once we understand about the pernicious nature of institutional racism, we can never recover the comfortable position of ignorance. We have bought a one-way ticket and there is no return—we can only move forward" (1983, p. 77).

COMMITMENT #2. Examine how we as individuals participate in our own oppression and the oppression of others by unconsciously mirroring the oppressive relations of the larger society.

This commitment on behalf of children requires us to acknowledge and take personal responsibility for our own beliefs and actions. Again, questions such as those listed here, when pursued within groups of people who trust and respect each other, may help adults recognize and analyze their own ethnocentrism.

By accepting that our society discriminates against and stereotypes people, we can better understand the realities of the lives of the children we teach.

- Do we expect children with stay-at-home mothers to be better nurtured than children whose parent(s) work?

- How do we respond to jokes that poke fun at people for their religion, race, ethnic group, nationality, or other characteristic? What do we say to comments such as, "I don't notice skin color. Everyone's the same to me"?

- Why do we use common phrases, holiday greeting cards, posters, or worksheets that depict stereotypes?

- How do we handle children's questions about skin color, clothing, hairstyles, language, or abilities?

Only through honest self-examination can we root out the prejudices that we have learned, practiced, and intentionally or inadvertently passed on to children.

Experiences past and present—stories read as children, TV and movie images, holiday celebrations, statements made by friends and acquaintances—constantly shape our beliefs. Many times, our experiences enable us to become more appreciative of the marvels of human diversity, but not always.

Research reveals, for instance, that many teachers are biased against either males or females, as well as African American children, lower-socioeconomic-status (lower-SES) children, and children with different abilities (Curry & Johnson, 1990). By accepting these common oppressive biases, teachers erode opportunities to nurture the next generation. When even one child is diminished in any way, all children are diminished, as is our effectiveness as teachers.

Education about all types of diversity, as conceived here, is *not* a self-esteem booster treatment for children who are considered to be oppressed or culturally different or disabled; rather, this approach to teaching is designed to help each of us overcome the tendency to harbor demeaning attitudes about some differences, while placing a positive value on others. Neither mainstream America nor any other culture or group is the center of the universe.

Young children are curious about their commonalties, their diversity, and their interwoven heritages. In every classroom, children and educators can put into daily practice the values Americans and others in the free world share: democracy, respect, free speech, truth, justice, and harmony. Children who learn in a democratic atmosphere will gain the perspec-

When even one child is diminished in any way, all children are diminished.

tives and knowledge they need to make wise decisions (Hendrick, 1992; Perry & Fraser, 1993). Perhaps eventually, the violence and oppression that have characterized our national and international past can be laid to rest.

COMMITMENT #3. To truly understand what culture means to a group of people, to understand how culture is a source of group power and strength, and to examine how to allow groups to retain their cultural integrity while they gain the skills to function in the larger society.

Again, looking at our own lives and then attempting to put ourselves in others' shoes are good ways to consider how to meet these three interwoven challenges.

- What does our culture mean to us? Why and how do we celebrate important events? How would we feel if our language, or clothing, or cherished values were ignored or ridiculed?

- What aspects of other cultures make us feel comfortable? Which characteristics tend to tip us off balance? Consider attributes such as history, language, music, dress, art, literature, religion, childrearing styles, and values.

- Which cultural values and behaviors must be preserved to enable children from any culture to maintain their sense of integrity, personal history, and meaning of life?

  - What additional skills and perspectives might some children need if they are to function successfully in broader society?

Most young children function quite well at home and in their own neighborhoods. They are relaxed,

The greater the disparity between home and school, the greater the anxiety for children.

have friends, and feel as though they have some control over their lives. They have spent five or more years learning from people who understand what matters in their community. Then comes enrollment in kindergarten or first grade. White and Siegel describe how it feels for children:

> It is the somewhat pleasant, but scary, destiny of small children to be faced constantly with the task of going to where they have never been before, of meeting and dealing with people they have never seen before, of doing things they have never done before. In a new environment, they have to arrive at emotional and social settlements before they begin to enter into the problems and processes of intellectual problem solving. They have to ask, "Is it safe here?" "Can somebody like me be here?" "Can I trust the people here?" "Can I trust myself to manage what I have to?" (1984, p. 253)

The greater the disparity between home and school, the greater the anxiety for children. How can teachers smooth this frightening transition for young children? By approximating familiar aspects of the local community in our classrooms—by aligning home and school

---

Teachers who develop curricula based on trust and respect

1. examine how American society perpetuates racism and oppression in subtle yet systematic ways;
2. recognize how individuals unconsciously mirror this oppression;
3. enable cultural groups to retain their integrity while they gain skills to function in the larger society; and
4. use their influence to change oppressive systems.

(Based on Phillips, 1988)

(Pechman, 1992)—teachers demonstrate genuine respect for children and their families (Hale, 1991). "Children learn best when their physical needs are met and they feel psychologically safe and secure" (NAEYC & NAECS/SDE, 1991, p. 25).

In a genuinely diverse classroom, all children are empowered as learners. We know from long-term research that children who get off to a sound educational start during their impressionable early years are far more likely to become productive, responsible adults (Lazar & Darlington, 1982; Lally, Mangione, Honig, & Wittmer, 1988; Weikart, 1989). Culture is the most powerful vehicle for learning because culture is the child's very being.

In a genuinely diverse classroom, all children are empowered as learners.

Effective educators are well-informed about, sensitive to, and responsive to cultural differences. They tune in to the local community. Children, families, and educators thus get to know each other in the spirit of building strength through their differences. Even seemingly minor attributes—hairstyles, names used for relatives, or recreational choices—are important indicators of a family's treasures. Some individuals, families, and cultures are boisterous; others are sedate. Some rush about; others are more laid back. Some cultures expect children to avert their eyes when talking to adults and never to ask questions; others foster bold forwardness in their children. If such variety didn't exist within and between people and their cultures, how dull life would be!

How do schools preserve these precious cultural differences and still make it possible for people to live and work peaceably, side by side? Teachers can select classroom resources, teaching strategies, and curriculum ideas that draw from the vast range of human experience, that merge classrooms with communities, and that enable children to truly think and to solve real problems in creative, respectful ways. That's the essence of valuing diversity.

Without this alignment between home and school cultures, overcoming the resulting mutual mistrust and alienation is exceedingly difficult (Comer, 1988a, b). The nation's alarming school drop-out rates attest to the lack of meaningful, confidence-inspiring education for children, even of those in the mainstream (First & Carrera, 1988). We must act now before more members of the next generation are set adrift by a system that harbors institutional racism.

COMMITMENT #4. Use our power to change the oppressive systems that exist in our society.

Inequities have been perpetrated, at one time or another, on nearly every group of people who call themselves Americans. Most teachers have probably heard Phillips's account of

> a story often told about a woman walking beside a river who hears the cry of a drowning man. She jumps into the river, pulls the man to the shore, and revives him. Soon, she hears another cry for help, and again, jumps into the river to save the victim. No sooner has she pulled the second man out than she hears another cry. And so it goes all day long, our woman pulling one drowning person after another out of the river. At day's end, exhausted, she sits down beside the river to rest, and realizes that she never

once stopped to go upstream to find out who was pushing people in. (1988, p. 47)

Educators who promote bright futures for children rush upstream to stop the discriminatory systems within and beyond the schools—whether they be the testing establishment, curriculum writers, school boards, legislators, vendors, or politicians. As activists, we can use our individual and collective power to call for "equal access to opportunities for education, jobs, housing, health, and growth-enhancing family lives" (Phillips, 1988).

At the same time, we must be realistic about what we can achieve in the classroom. "Schools alone cannot (nor should they be asked to) make up for all the barriers children face at society's hands. They can, however, create opportunities for children to overcome hurdles" (Pechman, 1992, p. 30). Educators can be the standard bearers for human rights and democracy in school *and* go beyond to work on the problems in society. The strength and future of our country, even the world, depend on optimal development of our most precious resource—our children.

We must examine these four commitments before we implement a curriculum that integrates and values diversity. We may need to reframe our perspectives about differences before teaching can be effective, and we must continue to return to these ethical commitments as experience in dealing with cultures sheds new light on the impact these commitments have on children.

Chapter 3

Criteria for Learning Materials and Activities

Most primary teachers have closets full of posters, photographs, books, games, patterns, computer programs, learning-center materials, and bulletin-board ideas. All of these items and ideas are still valuable in a diverse curriculum, although perhaps not quite in the way they were originally intended.

The guidelines offered here are posed as questions to help teachers evaluate how well typical teaching resources—materials and activities—convey respect for the dignity of children and their families. Experiences and items that meet these criteria are more likely to encourage development of the skills, attitudes, and knowledge that are the foundation for future learning and good citizenship (NAEYC, 1986; NAESP, 1990; NAEYC & NAECS/SDE, 1991, for detailed curriculum guidelines and assessment strategies that reflect developmentally appropriate practice).

Many excellent commercial and teacher-made learning resources are developmentally appropriate for most young children. Others are easily tailored to children's individual needs and interests. Many of these fine materials and activities have already become an integral part of primary classrooms.

Unfortunately, many other handy resources fail to meet these high standards necessary to convey respect. Do not throw out the rejects; instead, use these less appropriate items—with sensitive guidance—to enable children to discern differences between stereotyped and authentic portrayals of people.

With this knowledge, children in classrooms that cherish human rights and democratic ideals can then begin to counteract discrimination by writing letters to publishers or manufacturers, talking to government or school officials, refusing to read a book that pokes fun at a group of people, and standing up for what is fair whenever the occasion arises.

During a name-calling incident on the bus, for example, a child in such a democratic classroom might defend another, not with fists, but with reason: "People are not for teasing. Calling kids names hurts their feelings." Children will continue to use these skills as adults when they try to determine truth in advertising, evaluate the validity of news stories, ascertain a politician's stand, or consider the message perpetrated by the name of a sports team.

Apply these guidelines whenever new classroom materials or teaching strategies are chosen so teachers can ensure that commonly portrayed negative images are offset by a preponderance of high-quality, developmentally appropriate, antibias curriculum activities for children.

GUIDELINE #1. Do children learn primarily by extending their own experiences and gaining insights from each other? Does the activity or material make sense to them?

People of all ages—but especially young children—learn best when they start with what they already know and then have opportunities to expand upon their ideas and experiences, a process sometimes called *scaffolding* (Fischer & Bullock, 1984). Curriculum content worth knowing (NAEYC & NAECS/SDE, 1991) and that is appealing to children's interests will more likely remain relevant and thus remembered than will fragmented bits of nonsense.

Children are anthropologists who begin to learn about their heritages and values within their own families (Weitzman, 1975; Wolfman, 1991); they branch outward to learn about their friends as they mature: "If diverse cultures are represented in the classroom, the teacher will find a wealth of opportunities to help children become aware of cultural differences and to understand that no culture is better or worse than any other" (Little Soldier, 1989, p. 89). In these classrooms children are not mere tourists, getting an occasional superfluous glimpse of something unusual; they are immersed in the relevance of culture and other human characteristics in their daily lives (see Table 2).

Children who work together to prepare their friends' favorite family foods, build replicas of different types of contemporary homes, or hear descriptions

---

Table 2. Watch Out for the Signs of a Tourist Curriculum

Trivializing: Organizing activities only around holidays or only around food; only involving parents for holiday and cooking activities.

Tokenism: Having one Black doll amid many White dolls; a bulletin board of "ethnic" images—the only diversity in the room; only one book about any cultural group.

Disconnecting cultural diversity from daily classroom life: Reading books about children of color only on special occasions; teaching a unit on a different culture and then never seeing that culture again.

Stereotyping: Showing images of Native Americans all from the past; people of color always shown as poor; people from cultures outside the United States only shown in "traditional" dress and in rural settings.

Misrepresenting American ethnic groups: Treating books and pictures about life in Mexico as equivalent to the culture of Mexican Americans; doing activities based on Mexican American culture to teach about families from El Salvador or Guatemala or Nicaragua.

From *Anti-Bias Curriculum: Tools for Empowering Young Children* (p. 63) by L. Derman-Sparks & the A.B.C. Task Force, 1989, Washington, DC: NAEYC. Copyright © 1989 by Louise Derman-Sparks. Table revised 1993 by L. Derman-Sparks and printed by permission.

(sometimes in children's home languages) of each other's family photos find much that's familiar to them. Comments such as, "Hey, my grandmother lives at our house, too!" or "Our family likes to play a game like bocce, but we call it bowling," are indicators that children are building bridges between each other. They are indeed making sense of their world.

Memorizing facts, such as dates or the names of capital cities, on the other hand, is a waste of time at any age. Dates are only meaningful when children have developed a concept of the passage of time and understand the importance of the events (Seefeldt, 1975). This doesn't mean that young children can't learn geography or forge their own time frames, but they assimilate information better when they use these facts for a purpose in generating their own sense of history.

Knowing the name of a city and country is useful, for example, if a classmate's aunt and uncle live there and the group can write letters to them and exchange information. Children could find out how long it takes to fly or drive to the area, what the climate is like, what kinds of jobs people hold, what their clothing is like, which languages are spoken, and much other information to compare with their local community.

Many teachers find they stick to their goals for children more closely if they ask themselves these questions for every activity or material:

- What are children *really* learning by this experience?

> ### For every activity, ask
> - What are children *really* learning by this experience?
> - Does it have a meaningful purpose for children—does it make sense to them?

- Does it have a meaningful purpose for children—does it make sense to them?

Whatever the project, learning is enhanced if children can identify something familiar that they can latch onto and then work—usually individually or by collaborating in small groups—to build on what they know.

GUIDELINE #2. Can children carry out nearly all of the activity themselves?

Curricula that truly respect children's intelligence center on projects and themes that children can accomplish by themselves as industrious learners. Lack of opportunity to achieve *real* success on their own at school jeopardizes children's self-esteem and their desire to stay in school. Schoolwide multicultural fairs, for example, make marvelous events for faculty and families, but if adults do most of the work, children are robbed of enriching opportunities to work and learn together. Education is not a spectator sport—it is a social learning process.

Wise parents and teachers find a way to involve every child in major events such as fine arts programs or year-end celebrations. Even the youngest children can vote to select a theme, compile lists of materials needed, construct props, prepare snacks from many cultures, make tickets, and distribute programs. First graders who are learning about money might be cashiers; others could set up chairs or greet guests. A few of the second graders could design signs or read poetry in their home language while others carry boxes of supplies or manage other tasks. Older children take part according to their abilities and interests, too, sometimes assisting younger ones. Everyone contributes to the success of every occasion.

Daily classroom activities—yes, even those labeled *systematic instruction*—also can immerse children completely in their own learning when the activities are structured to engage children's thinking. Chil-

> **Classrooms that respect children's differences proudly display children's original artwork, creative writings, and other cooperative and individual efforts so that everyone can appreciate their true accomplishments.**

dren are always willing to tackle new challenges. They are curious. They get excited about learning. The teacher's role is to capitalize on this energy.

"We built our whole school with blocks. Look, here is our room," proudly exclaims Teixeira, who just a few months ago spoke only a few words of English. The construction is recorded with a nearby camera; the photos will be added to the classroom book. Teixeira and her friends may dictate or write a story about their work so that other children can read about what they did.

Inspired by the construction, some children might draw a floor plan or share an opportunity of seeing the blueprints of the building. Perhaps an excursion to the school's utility room would add another dimension, or the neighborhood could spring up around the school as the children use more blocks to add more buildings. The entire project might be preserved by using discarded boxes, glue, and other art materials to construct a replica. Streets, cars, buses, playgrounds, trees, classmates' homes, stores—how much there is to explore!

Classrooms that respect children's differences proudly display children's original artwork, creative writings, and other cooperative and individual efforts so that everyone can appreciate their true accomplishments. Progress is measured in terms of sensible goals reached by each child. Evidence of children's progress—their very own masterpieces, untouched by adult interference—covers the school's walls and halls.

Mindless activities such as "workbooks, patterns, and cutting and tracing lines [are] largely a waste of children's time," contend Katz and Chard (1989, p. ix). If school doesn't make sense to children, they'll wander aimlessly, interrupt others, or ignore what's assigned because everything looks like something they did before. None of their seven intelligences will be inspired.

Conversely, when children experience real successes in diverse environments, they grow as increasingly involved and responsible members of their classroom and community. Children immersed in learning rarely exhibit discipline problems—they're too busy to goof off!

Young children can become engrossed in doing their own personal research with picture books, making visits to a historical site, or conducting informal interviews of friends or relatives. Ask a second grade class, for example, to find out how and when their families first came to the United States. Explore who might be able to tell them. Some children might use a tape recorder, others could write notes. Where might they find more information? What memorabilia exists from those early days?

Some children may discover that their parents flew here on a plane when an older sibling was age three, or learn their ancestors walked southward across the

> **Children learn when their hearts, hands, and minds are engaged.**

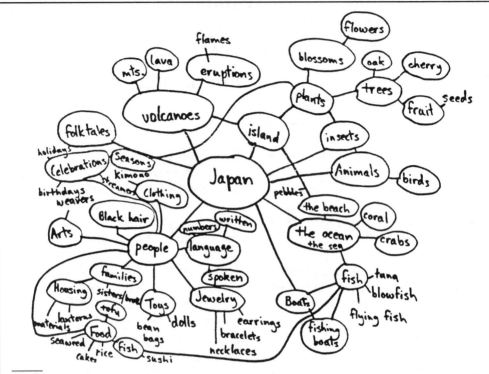

Figure 1. Example of a Web Approach to Developing Ideas About a Topic

continent thousands of years ago. The story for others may describe family brought here against their will in America's colonial days or arriving on an immigrant ship at Ellis Island or Angel Island at the turn of the century. One by one, each helped America grow into a political and economic world power.

Chart on maps the families' departure and arrival points, moves, and location where the children live now. Construct on the playground a timeline of arrivals. How many miles have their families traveled? Why did they settle here? Perhaps a relative could sing a few traditional songs with friends at school. Language arts, math, science, history, art, music—the possibilities are endless for stretching children's varied intelligences.

Children learn when their hearts, hands, and minds are engaged (Katz & Chard, 1989). Ideas branch out much like spider webs—that is how teachers and children jointly develop classroom projects and identify their outcomes (Workman & Anziano, 1993). One example is how a first grade class pursued its interest in Japan (Figure 1). Using a web approach, one topic leads to another; children take off to explore their own particular interests, and all the traditional subjects intermingle in meaningful ways. Everyone plunges into learning with verve!

GUIDELINE #3. Do culture and history come alive?

The best learning materials and activities authentically capture real-life people, adventures, beliefs, and conditions that led to events and ideas. Teachers who eagerly delve into their own understanding of how the United States has evolved—from immigration to Manifest Destiny to Puerto Rican statehood, from slavery to immigrant labor to build the railroads to equal opportunity employers—will pass on their curiosity and history's relevance to the youngest of children. To obtain a truer picture of all that has happened, locate information presented from varied viewpoints, compared to material limited to a Eurocentric perspective.

Reading together biographies and historical fiction—such as the Laura Ingalls Wilder stories (1953), *Turquoise Boy* (Cohlene, 1990), or *The Olden Days* (Mathieu, 1979)—leaves young children spellbound, especially when the stories are supplemented with hands-on artifacts. Select photographs of people and their surroundings, unprocessed wool to be carded, tortillas to mix and shape, Navajo blankets to wrap around themselves, or old-fashioned games to make and play. Storytellers, puppets, dioramas, hands-on history museums, cooking, gardening, films, or computer simulation games are just some of the means to bring everyday heroes and heroines to life—and up to the present—for children.

Stay alert to erroneous information and stereotypes in stories and illustrations, especially in older books that are viewed as classics (Wilder's portrayal of Native Americans as naked, for example, in *On the Banks of Plum Creek*). Encourage children to think about why people held biased ideas. Together, seek out what was and is more accurate.

The grizzled Mountain Man—dressed in buckskin—holds groups of 3- to 93-year-olds at rapt attention for an hour as he tells tales of the Appalachians in the days of a century or two ago. Gifted storytellers such as this former teacher draw the audience into the drama. "All right, all you critters . . . ," he addresses the children as he begins. One young boy's eyes widen like saucers as the storyteller waves a five-foot long, scraggly stick during a yarn about a wise American Indian. Children sit on carpet squares, transfixed by the humor and suspense. Wiggly? No way! These children are immersed in history!

Experiences involving real people, visits to neighborhood stores, and other lively experiences—such as those described throughout this classroom guide—help to counteract the negative, stereotypical images of Native Americans and immigrant groups who arrived on America's shores centuries later. Invite children into the cultures and histories of their own families/peoples—many children will have two or more—and those of their friends and neighbors (Root, 1992).

GUIDELINE #4. Are people's real experiences—clothing, habits, music, homes, families, foods, capabilities, preferences, ages—accurately portrayed?

Accurate and fair portrayals of many cultures and individuals are still difficult to locate, although recent materials tend to be somewhat more relevant and sensitive to people's feelings and history than works published before the Civil Rights Movement (CIBC, n.d.). Publishers who specialize in culturally relevant materials are usually reliable sources (see Part 3), but teachers still need to exercise care in making sure the materials are good matches for what children already know and to their need for concrete, hands-on learning.

Children can develop critical thinking skills as they evaluate how an illustration

Invite children into the cultures and histories of their own families/peoples, and those of their friends and neighbors.

might make someone feel, consider whether features on a doll or puppet are authentic, or discuss whether a story's plot, language, or characters are realistic. Together, teachers and children can search for

- authenticity instead of stereotypes;
- aesthetically pleasing, realistic, and yet distinctive drawings of ethnic people or persons with impairments (instead of illustrations exaggerating features or showing European-looking faces, skin, and hair textures that merely have been shaded red, beige, brown, or black);
- contemporary as well as historical treatments;
- heroines or heroes worth admiring;
- everyday lives featured more often than special occasions;
- materials written and illustrated by people of the culture or group being described, and in their native language occasionally;
- story plots that demonstrate people working together (rather than glorifying violence and war); and
- terminology that is current and positive (rather than condescending, patronizing, or dehumanizing such as *savage, primitive,* or *I is for Indian*).

Weed out materials that perpetrate myths or that portray insulting images, and use them in teaching children "to recognize stereotypes and caricatures of different groups" (Derman-Sparks, Gutiérrez, & Phillips, 1989, p. 3). Table 3 summarizes some commonly perpetrated myths that are dispelled in the Americans All materials and elsewhere as indicators of the type of unfair, untrue information that has prevailed about the various cultural groups who live in the United States.

GUIDELINE #5. Are a variety of cultures and human characteristics included, with emphasis on the peoples who live within the children's community? Are people viewed as unique individuals within a culture?

Legends and similar reminders of the past are marvelous teaching tools now and then, but as a steady diet they may suggest to young children that these cultures are frozen in time, or that they no longer exist. Overemphasis on rural settlers or pioneers ignores the fact that many immigrants came to—and stayed in—America's burgeoning cities.

Contemporary—as well as historical—people and their lives demand portrayal if children are to fully comprehend the march of human history and its relevance to life now. Children who know real people—from a variety of cultures and age groups, and with varying capabilities—are far more likely to expect fairness as a way of life for all within democracy. They soon recognize that people within any group are not all alike, and begin to see each person as an important individual.

Demonstrate that diversity is valued by helping children get acquainted with school staff, medical personnel, service workers, local leaders, and many people within the community. Encourage children to attend interesting events with their families, and schedule frequent classroom guests and field trips. In addition, display pictures of women and

Make sure materials are good matches for what children already know and to their need for concrete, hands-on learning.

Table 3. Distinguishing Myth From Reality

Native Americans

Myth: Columbus discovered America in 1492.

Reality: Native Americans walked from Asia to the continent of North America as long as 30,000 years before Columbus landed here. There were about 10 million people—speaking 350 different languages—living on this continent in the late 1400s.

Myth: The first Thanksgiving was a Pilgrim and Indian feast of rejoicing.

Reality: A feast of Thanksgiving likely never happened. "Many Native American groups regard Thanksgiving as a Day of Mourning. . . . For them, it is a symbol of the Europeans' first foothold on the North American continent and the demise of the Native way of life" (Ramsey, 1979, p. 29).

Myth: Indians were savages who scalped settlers.

Reality: Native Americans were kind to the new arrivals, and taught them how to survive in the wilderness. They shared their medicines, and helped immigrants to build shelters and canoes with trees. They introduced foods to the Europeans—turkeys, maple sugar, corn, beans, squash, sunflowers, and pumpkins. They taught newcomers how to farm this soil and how to dry foods to preserve them. The First Americans showed how to mine precious metals from the ground. The democratic principles of the Iroquois government probably influenced the content of the U.S. Constitution. In return the Europeans shared their metal tools, cloth, guns, sheep, goats, and horses with the Native Americans.

Myth: The U.S. government has been generous with Native Americans.

Reality: As European immigrants spread out across America, they took over the fields, pastures, forests, and hunting and fishing areas that had been cared for by Native Americans for generations. The Indians lost about a billion acres—often in fierce battles—and were forced onto reservations unsuitable for farming or hunting.

The U.S. government signed at least 380 treaties with the Native Americans and broke nearly every one. The needs and rights of Indians were often ignored or even trampled on by the Bureau of Indian Affairs. The First Americans were not considered U.S. citizens until 1924. Indian children were taken from their homes and sent to schools in an effort to replace Indian languages and cultures with White American ways. Today, the U.S. government is making efforts to repair the enduring effects of the broken treaties.

African Americans

Myth: All Africans were brought to America as slaves.

Reality: Archaeological clues in Central and South America indicate that African explorers and traders may have arrived in this hemisphere before the Europeans. Some Africans came with the Spanish explorers as soldiers and guides. About 15 million slaves were brought here between 1600 and 1800. After slavery was abolished, millions of free Black immigrants came to this country—many to northern industrial cities—to look for jobs. In the early 1900s, about 500,000 immigrants arrived at Ellis Island from Africa and the Caribbean.

Asian Americans

Myth: Asian immigrants were easily assimilated into U.S. culture.

Reality: Chinese, Japanese, Filipinos, and immigrants from countries such as Vietnam, Thailand, and Korea often have been lumped together as a group, but their histories, cultures, and experiences in this country are very different. Until the 1960s, most Asian immigrants were treated unfairly by immigration and other discriminatory laws.

Chinese. The economy in China was wavering as gold was being discovered in California; few Chinese miners remained in the mines due to discrimination. Thousands of Chinese workers labored in the 1860s—at lower wages than Whites—to build the western part of the U.S. transcontinental railroad.

---

*Based on materials from a variety of sources including Americans All.

Anti-Chinese sentiments prevailed for years; from 1882 until 1943, only a few Chinese students, teachers, and merchants were allowed to come to this country.

Japanese. Hawaii's sugar plantations drew the first large wave of Japanese immigrants in the 1880s, but racist laws in California and tight immigration laws limited the number who entered the mainland. Japanese immigrants, mostly men, were only allowed to marry other Japanese—a restriction that led to the dehumanizing practice of selecting brides chosen from pictures. During World War II, the U.S. government sent many Japanese Americans to detention camps in this country.

Filipinos. Some Filipino immigrants came to America in the late 1800s, but when Spain transferred the Philippine Islands to the United States at the end of the Spanish-American War in 1898, Filipinos became U.S. nationals who could enter the country at any time. Most Filipino immigrants experienced discrimination. Some were mistaken for Japanese Americans and sent to detention camps in World War II. In 1946, the Philippines became an independent nation.

Europeans

Myth: Most European immigrants came to America to escape religious persecution.

Reality: Religious persecution brought Pilgrim and Puritan families here, but many European immigrants came for other reasons: adventure, dreams of riches, belief in freedom, jobs, escape from famine or overcrowded homelands, gain of land for farming, relief from taxes. Between 1600 and 1800, about half of the immigrants came as indentured servants (they agreed to work a given number of years for the person who paid their boat fare).

Upon arrival, many Europeans witnessed continued oppression for their religious beliefs, experienced government by aristocrats who "thought that democracy was the 'meanest and worst' of all forms of government" (Bailey, 1966, p. 27), found difficulty in securing jobs, and paid taxes without representation.

Mexican Americans

Myth: Mexican Americans are newcomers to the U.S. southwest.

Reality: In 1521 Spain invaded and defeated the Aztecs—who had long lived in what is now Mexico—and enslaved the Indians and exposed them to European diseases. Within 150 years, so few Native Americans remained that African slaves were brought to Mexico. The three cultural groups intermarried and are the ancestors of today's Mexicans.

Land disputes in the U.S. southwest have played a major role in the fate of Mexican Americans. Before it became a state, Texas was part of both Mexico and the United States and an independent republic. New Mexico, California, Nevada, Utah, and parts of Colorado, Wyoming, and Arizona were ceded from Mexico to the United States in 1848, and suddenly many Mexicans became residents of the United States. These Mexicans were frequently treated as a conquered people, and discrimination was common. Mexican miners were driven out of the gold camps by discriminatory laws and violence. Mexican farmers and ranchers were forced off their lands by the railroads. They resorted to migrant work at low wages. Many Mexicans still find themselves welcome only when the United States needs cheap labor.

Puerto Ricans

Myths: Puerto Rico is an independent country; Puerto Rico is like a U.S. state.

Reality: Puerto Rico is a U.S. commonwealth, or self-governing U.S. possession. Puerto Ricans are U.S. citizens who elect a governor and rule themselves under their own constitution. Their representative in the U.S. Congress cannot vote. Puerto Ricans living in Puerto Rico can vote only in local elections, not for members of Congress or for the president; those who live in the United States can vote in all U.S. elections. Puerto Ricans pay U.S. taxes and serve in the armed forces. Some hope that Puerto Rico will become the fifty-first state.

Myth: Puerto Ricans are the same as Mexicans.

Reality: The Puerto Rican people are a blend of the island's original Taino Indians and settlers from Spain, Portugal, France, and Italy. Puerto Ricans have their own unique Caribbean culture.

men of all ages and from different ethnic groups engaged in jobs that are familiar to most children—postal workers, police officers, retail personnel, medical staff. Choose toy figures and puppets that accurately represent several features of our humanity.

Children who know real people are far more likely to expect fairness as a way of life.

Language shapes how we think, and the influx of recent immigrants from hundreds of linguistic backgrounds presents a unique challenge to American schools. Although some earlier immigrant groups sought to homogenize themselves into the English-speaking culture here, many parents today prefer to preserve their language heritage through their children. It is also important that children maintain their ability to communicate with their families.

Children who are not native-English speakers will eventually need to learn English if they are to thrive in this country, and may become fluent in two or more languages, as is common in industrialized European countries and Japan. Children can switch from one language at home to another at school, as is evidenced by the variety of dialects and colloquialisms most Americans already use in varying circumstances.

Learning to sign a few fragmented vocabulary words, to sing one song in French, or to identify a few Braille letters is linguistic tokenism that demeans people's abilities or cultures. Books, texts, recordings, games, and children's writings should reflect the diversity of language within the community. Kendall cautions teachers to "Look carefully at the use of dialect. Is it genuine or is it fabricated?" (1983, p. 60). Look for books generated by speakers and artists who are part of the group described; translations, for example, often miss the broader context in which a story takes place.

Respect children's home languages and incorporate them into the school as children gradually learn to function in English. "Research suggests that whole language activities may be helpful in furthering both oral and written English language development of LEP [limited English-proficient] students" (Abramson, Seda, & Johnson, 1990, p. 69).

Encourage children to read and write in the language in which they most comfortably communicate. They can teach each other (and their teachers) useful phrases and beloved songs in their own languages. Families might be asked to share magazines, newspapers, or other printed material with the class. In a classroom that is filled with lively literacy experiences—print materials and plenty of opportunities for children to talk, play, and work together—children will naturally achieve greater communicative competence and the ability to see each other as individuals.

What if a classroom or community appears to be homogeneous? Extra efforts are needed—perhaps adopting a Sister School (Koeppel & Mulrooney, 1992)—to ensure children's familiarity with other populations (Table 6). Often, even people who appear to be similar actually are quite diverse—just ask about their favorite music, or clothing styles, or authors, or foods.

Respect children's home languages and incorporate them into the school as children gradually learn to function in English.

Table 4. Caution

All children need to see people like themselves in abundance in their classrooms, as well as be exposed to the range of diversity among humans; however, the impact of the various institutional "isms," such as racism, on the images in our society (e.g., in the media) and on the production and selection of materials for early childhood programs means that some children are much more likely than others to see people like themselves.

- Those children *most likely* to see images of people who look and live like themselves are European American, middle or upper–middle class, able-bodied, or male, and live in two-parent, heterosexual families.

- Those children *least likely* to see images of people who look and live like themselves are children—of color; in interracial/interethnic families; with disabilities; or in families that are poor, homeless, single-parent, extended, or gay/lesbian headed.

Early childhood educators must take care to ensure that images of children and adults from the least-likely-to-see-themselves groups are amply and accurately represented.

From *Anti-Bias Curriculum: Tools for Empowering Young Children* (p. 13) by L. Derman-Sparks & the A.B.C. Task Force, 1989, Washington, DC: NAEYC. Copyright © 1989 by Louise Derman-Sparks. Table revised 1993 by L. Derman-Sparks and printed by permission.

GUIDELINE #6. Is pride in each child's heritage fostered?

Some people believe that through culturally focused materials and activities children develop an inflated sense of superiority about themselves and their culture. Such a tragic educational misuse is indeed possible, as evidenced by our country's long and tenacious history of prejudice against people who appear non-European. Other individuals believe that cultural materials only point out differences that can aggravate dislikes among children. A balanced, respectful, integrated educational approach—such as that advocated here—never sets one culture or group above another, but rather helps children gradually and naturally learn to appreciate diversity within and among cultures and all peoples. The time is always right to nurture truth, self-esteem, and pride in *all* children, *all* people, as individuals with their own unique attributes (Table 4).

Each of us is a product of at least one culture. We all get hungry, need a place to live, love our families and friends, seek productive work, and learn what our culture deems to be important. These are the

A balanced, respectful, integrated educational approach never sets one culture or group above another, but rather helps children gradually and naturally learn to appreciate the value of diversity within and among cultures.

starting points for young children to naturally learn about cultures and how to achieve harmony with each other in a democratic country.

A balanced, respectful, integrated educational approach never sets one culture above another, but rather helps children gradually and naturally learn to appreciate the value of diversity within and among cultures.

GUIDELINE #7. Are principles of democracy instilled?

Today democracy shines so brightly around the world, as peoples struggle for—and sometimes gain—the freedoms that for so long have been denied to them. The fall of the Berlin Wall opened up new hope for many oppressed peoples, but Americans also cannot take their rights and responsibilities for granted, nor assume all in the United States are equally free.

When children experience democracy as a way of life, they grow in their commitment to all the lofty ideals—truth, justice, free speech, equal opportunity, voting privileges, human rights—that the Constitution of the United States upholds. Using teaching materials and strategies that integrate concepts of respect, human diversity, and democracy is essential if children are to become self-motivated, self-controlled problem solvers and the leaders of the twenty-first century.

Criteria for learning materials and activities

1. Do children learn primarily by extending their own experiences and gaining insights from each other? Does the activity or material make sense to them?
2. Can children carry out nearly all of the activity themselves?
3. Do culture and history come alive?
4. Are people's real experiences—clothing, habits, music, homes, families, foods, capabilities, preferences, ages—accurately portrayed? Are people viewed as unique individuals within a culture?
5. Are a variety of cultures portrayed, with emphasis on the peoples who live within the children's community?
6. Is pride in each child's heritage fostered?
7. Are principles of democracy instilled?

First, we turn to specifics about some of these materials. Then, in Part 2 we explore the primary teaching methods—democratic conflict resolution (McCracken, 1990; Carlsson-Paige & Levin, 1992), positive discipline (Nelsen, 1987), an antibias curriculum (Derman-Sparks & the A.B.C. Task Force, 1989), and cooperative learning (Kohn, 1991; Slavin, 1991)—that can help ensure children's commitment to our country's democratic way of life for its diverse peoples.

Using teaching materials and strategies that integrate respect, human diversity, and democracy is essential if children are to become self-motivated, self-controlled problem solvers and the leaders of the twenty-first century.

Chapter 4

Preparing a Diverse Environment

Each year, the group personality is a bit different as new children enter a kindergarten, first, or second grade class. Every year, though, familiarity and balance are the keys to creating a classroom that welcomes children and invites them to be comfortable as they eagerly go about learning through developmentally and individually appropriate experiences. The teacher's warmth and insights are evident in all that is absorbed from—and takes place in—the classroom.

Concentrate on bringing topics to life—in a way that integrates the curriculum, whether it's science, reading, spelling, language arts, math, music, art, physical education, or social studies—with an abundance of hands-on cultural artifacts, mobility aids, foods, and everyday stuff. In classrooms that celebrate diversity, children encounter objects, ideas, and people that make them feel at home from the moment they first walk through the door. Select items such as these from the world's marketplace:

- pillows, rugs, and wall hangings;
- baskets made from many materials;
- lacquered boxes, wooden bowls, hollowed-out gourds;
- wind chimes, drums, and other authentic musical instruments, plus recordings of a variety of types of choral and instrumental music;
- sculpture and prints of fine art work;
- jewelry made from wooden beads, shells, turquoise, seeds, and other materials;
- puppets and dolls made from fabric, wood, china, plastic;
- stuffed, rubber, and wooden animals;
- pictures, magazines, and books;
- eating and cooking utensils;
- coins and paper money;
- plants and plant materials—such as cacti, ferns, and cotton—from different climates;
- tools for everyday living; and
- much more.

Collaborate with other teachers to accumulate a varied collection of these artifacts for the entire school, then rotate items. In this way a minimum amount of storage is needed, and costs are kept low.

In each classroom, every learning center, every wall, every shelf, every nook and cranny proclaims "All children are welcome here!" Within the first few hours of school, children's own art and writing spring up on the walls, as children transform the classroom into their own habitat. Some children might like to make a mural depicting the good times they had during the summer. Others could write individual stories about "My family likes to . . . " or "I wish I could . . . " or another theme that will begin to foster friendship and understanding.

Labels in two or more languages might be attached to pet cages, pencil sharpeners, and other objects. Posted friendly phrases in children's own languages can greet children upon return from recess. The wide variety of cultural and personal expressions convey the message that each child is valued, each ethnic group is important—no one feels put-on-the-spot or ignored. Everyone is competent!

Before many days have passed, children begin to feel at home with objects some of their friends already recognize from their own homes. "When we bring bits and pieces of the world into the daily life of our programs, the unfamiliar becomes familiar; what was outside our experience becomes part of our frame of reference," notes Neugebauer (1992, p. 16). Each item to handle, see, smell, hear, or taste leads children on to more learning that awaits them.

Because "there are no advertising standards for the promotion of educational products, or surgeon-general's warnings that the product could be dangerous to mental health" (Smith, 1986, p. 10), teachers must rely on their own professional judgment when tailoring classrooms to diverse children and their communities. The five educational goals for children (Chapter 1) and seven criteria for learning materials and activities (Chapter 3) are incorporated into questions to consider whenever selecting projects and specific materials (Table 5). Positive answers to these questions most likely indicate that the action or strategy supports the development of sound educational goals, and thus children's long-term development.

Textbooks, computer programs, and audiovisual materials

Nearly every so-called educational item on the market claims to be developmentally appropriate or multicultural, but how can everything be just right for every group of young children? Be skeptical! Slick packages particularly may claim they require no teacher preparation or other materials—that merely means that some business people believe that teachers are incapable of thinking for themselves or finding the time to do so.

Oftentimes the smaller publishers and suppliers carry the most authentic materials (see a listing in Part 3). What's more, these rarely advertised materials generally lend themselves far better to the flexibility required by teachers' imaginations and children's interests.

Insist on previewing everything before purchase. If items exist already in the school's collection, carefully examine

---

The wide variety of cultural and personal expressions convey that each child is valued, each ethnic group is important. Everyone is competent!

Table 5. Diversity in Our Lives: What Are Children *Really* Learning?

These questions offer a guide for selecting appropriate learning materials, teaching and parenting strategies, and activities for young children in programs and at home.

1. How well do pictures, posters, games, and other materials represent *real* people?
   a. Are people respectfully depicted as positive, active, considerate, and cooperative?
   b. Are the numbers of males and females balanced?
   c. Are people with a variety of physical and mental abilities depicted?
   d. Are people from various ethnic/cultural groups pictured in traditional and contemporary settings, dress, and hairstyles? Are facial features, skin tones, and other characteristics accurate? Are artifacts and information authentic?
   e. Are people of many ages represented?
   f. Are work activities, dwellings, natural resources, and families depicted with diversity?
   g. Do displays feature children's own original art work?
   h. Are materials placed where children can see and touch them?

2. How well do the messages in children's books and recordings—both individual titles and the collection as a whole—reflect reality?
   a. Are the characters and illustrations diverse (see *a* through *f* above)?
   b. Do characters speak and act like real people?
   c. Are text and illustrations accurate in their information?
   d. Are both historical and contemporary settings depicted?

   e. Are situations resolved in ways we expect children to emulate?
   f. Are children urged to think critically about what they read, hear, and see?

3. How are children encouraged to succeed?
   a. Do people, learning materials, toys, and activities reflect children's cultures and the world's peoples? Do children and families feel respected? Are people within the community seen as primary resources? Are differences resolved through discussion with families?
   b. Do adults have realistic, individualized expectations for children based on their ages, abilities, learning styles, family values, and life experiences?
   c. Are children taught—and expected to use—skills such as decision making, democratic conflict resolution, and acting to solve problems? Are children interested and absorbed in worthwhile activities?
   d. Do adults support children's curiosity, self-motivation, and desire to control themselves?
   e. Are various types of play offered (small-/large-motor, quiet/noisy, mostly child-directed/some adult-directed, individual/small group, cooperative/individual)? Are children encouraged to engage in a variety of activities?
   f. Are children urged to evaluate their own efforts and progress?

them before use, to avoid sudden surprises that might necessitate an unexpected change in the direction of children's learning. Use the seven criteria questions in Chapter 3 and those in Table 5 to determine how well each activity promotes sound educational goals for children. Note the date, graphics, vocabulary, expertise of the consultants on the project, and even the packaging.

"Too often the world is presented from a White, middle-class American point of view . . . . Cultural differences such as styles of dress or foods eaten are presented as foreign, quaint, or exotic. Presenting material in this manner encourages intolerance rather than openness in children," warns Kendall (1983, p. 63). When in doubt, call in experts—colleagues or school families whose cultural perspective is from the inside because the culture is theirs—to help determine whether the item reflects reality and fairness.

Review textbooks, workbooks, and worksheets for possible bias. Supplement these printed curriculum materials with an abundance of real-life items that more fully convey the topic. Textbooks, workbooks, and worksheets are probably the weakest of resources to inspire children's learning because often they are static—watering down ideas, portraying wooden characters, and failing to capture and engage more than one or two of children's seven intelligences. Most computer games are not much better; they're simply workbooks glorified by color and sound. Rote memory practice clearly is *not* the way young children learn—and remember—best.

Children will learn far more in using computers if teachers seek out computer games and simulations, for example, that spur children to make logical decisions and experience the consequences of their choices as the task unfolds (Haugland & Shade, 1988; Clements, Nastasi, & Swaminathan, 1993).

Supplement standard curriculum materials with real-life items that more fully convey the topic.

Computers can also make it easier for children to write their own stories, to edit their work, and to make the product available to others to enjoy. Unless children are accomplishing meaningful things—at the computer or on paper—their time could be far better spent doing something else.

Filmstrips, recordings, and videotapes are staples of every school, but must be used with caution to avert any possible ethnocentricity or outright stereotyping subtly or blatantly embedded in them. If necessary, rewrite sections of film or filmstrip narratives, or select just one song or portion of a recording; translate lyrics into children's own languages. New recordings are continually being released. Use Red Grammar's *Teaching Peace* (1986) or Ella Jenkins's numerous recordings in imaginative ways. Look for audiovisual materials produced by people whose culture is featured.

Prepare read-along books and tapes, using the children's writings or other culturally authentic works not yet converted into this popular format for beginning readers. Children can do practically everything: the reading, the cues for page-turning, the labeling of the cassette.

Sometimes, when budgets are limited, the best that can be done is to use the materials on hand, even if they are biased or outdated. Point out to children any distortions they may not recognize; encourage children to detect factual errors, inconsistencies, or stereotypes. Ask probing questions such as: What do you think is unfair in this story? How does this story differ from real life? Why do you think children live differently today? Which illustration(s) could hurt people's feelings? Why?

Don't stop with just alerting the children about biased materials. As Carol Phillips urged earlier (Chapter 2), go upstream, and try to stop whoever is pushing people in. As a class, write to the company and distributor to protest the stereotypes. Be specific about the problem. Document information. Suggest ways to make improvements. Ask for the courtesy of an answer. Send copies of the letter to the principal, the curriculum specialist, the librarian, and any other school staff members who should know about the concerns. Children will be so proud of themselves for standing up for what's right and fair, and will gain valuable critical thinking and consumer skills in the process.

Borrow more appropriate books and films from a library; write better materials; ask parents to loan authentic artifacts; plan for regular guests to share their heritage; engage children in creating replicas—textbooks should take a back seat to better, more appropriate ways to stimulate learning anyway.

Ask probing questions such as: What do you think is unfair in this story? How does this story differ from real life? Why do you think children live differently today? Which illustration(s) could hurt people's feelings? Why?

Children's books

Children's trade books are a vital part of the process of learning to read. All through the early years, parents and teachers who enthusiastically read to children several times each day find that their children are the ones who become the most avid readers. The selection of children's

> ## Stand up for what's right
>
> 1. Alert the children to biases in any materials. If necessary, explain what is more fair or accurate. Develop children's skills and knowledge to find factual errors, inconsistencies, or stereotypes.
> 2. As a class, write to the company and distributor to protest the stereotypes. Be specific about the problem. Document information. Suggest a reasonable solution. Request a response.
> 3. Send copies of the letter to the principal, the curriculum specialist, the librarian, purchasing agent, or any other school staff members who should know about the concerns.

literature, therefore, must be undertaken with the greatest of care, so that children early in their lives gain an appreciation for the articulate use of words from many languages and the value of fine art in conveying universal messages.

Children's books hold a wealth of fascinating information and inspiration, or serve as a vehicle for perpetuating myths and stereotypes, depending on the choice of content and how it is used. A hard lesson for many of us is learning that being published doesn't guarantee material that's true or fair, whether a picture book or an encyclopedia.

The Council on Interracial Books for Children once served as a watchdog organization for antibias materials, but as a consumer advocacy group was no match for those who put greed or hate above cherished democratic principles. Steer away from cartoon characters; poorly conceived illustrations; stories that patronize children (as in sing-song poetry); and dolls,

Select books more representative, more accurate, and positive in their portrayals of cultural heritages and today's diverse families and workforce.

toys, and other products that are commercials for movies or even theme parks. Write letters to protest the mindlessness and violence pervading many children's books.

Teachers are encouraged to work with school and local librarians to select books more representative, more accurate, and positive in their portrayals of cultural heritages and today's diverse families and workforce. Share the criteria and resources offered here; urge involvement of the community in the book-selection process. In addition to the criteria already established here, Neugebauer aptly offers two other practical guidelines that apply especially to children's literature:

- "They are good stories. They are interesting both to read and to listen to.
- The illustrations work with the text and in many, many instances are wonderfully delightful or breathtaking" (1992, p. 163).

A few children's books are listed in Part 3 as jumping-off points for locating high-quality children's literature that values diversity. Poetry, fiction, nonfiction, music books, collections of fingerplays, and any other material printed between two covers will be cherished for years by children as they discover new meanings in familiar books.

Reading extends children's thinking. *Swimmy* (Lionni, 1968) wonderfully illustrates the depth of messages that can be embedded in fine children's literature.

Lionni dramatically conveys the value of cooperation between fish of different colors; his simply elegant collage illustrations enhance the message. After reading picture books such as this, children might write or tell other stories about cooperation; or they might carve woodcuts or print designs by other simple processes, combining them with bits of paper doilies, lace, ribbon, or some paint, to create their own visions of the variety of life, at sea or within their neighborhoods.

Children who internalize fine literature through repeated readings and hands-on experiences remember enchanting picture books long after they become readers. In teaching, return again and again to authors, writers, and publishers who consistently strive to laud diversity and heighten children's sense of beauty and awe about the world.

There are many ways to make reading and writing a lively part of the day. Read with drama: whisper, shout, or look determined along with the characters. Stop midway in a story and ask children to predict the outcome. Insert common expressions from children's languages. Ask thought-provoking questions that begin with "Why ?" or "How ?" Urge children to get in on the action when motions and sounds are repeated. Tell stories with puppets, flannel boards, or without any props at all. Children might design costumes and sets to reenact a favorite story.

Compare similar stories from different cultures, or the same story as it has been interpreted by several translators and artists. For example, *The Mitten* is a Ukranian folk tale that has been retold and illustrated the world over (Tresselt, 1964; Botting, 1975; Brett, 1989). Search for similar themes such as animals, stars, lullabies, or storms, and explore how these ageless ideas are expressed in the art and literature of many cultures.

Invite local authors to talk about their books with children, or ask them to assist children with writing and editing their own materials. Schedule community leaders, including school administrators and board members, to come to the classroom to read to the children. Children who read widely are generally fine writers as well. Computers can be a boon for publishing class newsletters, stories, reports, thank-you notes, and announcements.

Art that picks up on themes or moods to illustrate a story is best created by children, rather than on the computer. Beware of clip art programs, stencils, coloring books, and other such materials that dampen children's creativity and sense of competence. Children's illustrations of their own stories can be executed

oping a program in which families honor a birthday child by donating a book or children's magazine subscription to the school in their child's name. Coordinate the idea with the school librarian, who might offer a list of new and welcome titles. If parents or other family members are available, invite them to read the gift book to the class on the child's birthday.

Implement regular book-exchange programs as another inexpensive way to promote reading. Children swap their old favorites for their friends' outgrown books. Parent-teacher organizations can organize the schoolwide event; children can promote the idea, bring in their books, sort them, help with distribution, and assist with cleanup. The same books can be recycled again and again. Publicity and enthusiasm for such events guarantee their success.

> Children who internalize fine literature through repeated readings and hands-on experiences remember enchanting picture books long after they become readers.

Reading fine children's books—together or in a quiet spot alone—is surely one of the best ways to incorporate diversity into every aspect of the curriculum. Real people and places spring to life on the book pages and become children's friends. Thanks to libraries, this fabulous resource can cost absolutely nothing and the selection can be conveniently varied.

in their choice of media: oil crayons, charcoal, tempera, papier maché, soap carvings, yarn, or clay, for example. Permit the work to be their own creation, not the teacher's or some stranger's idea.

Families are equally important in fostering children's love of reading. Urge parents to read with children at home, and in their family's preferred language. Suggest that older children read to younger children and to the whole family. Urge families to give books as gifts. Share story-hour information and recommended book lists. Keep the school library open, if possible, during long holiday breaks.

One terrific method for communicating the value of books to children is devel-

Games, puzzles, and other equipment

Learning possibilities abound when children play traditional and contemporary games. Think, for example, about the value of chasing games such as the Chinese game, Dragon's Tail, which is similar to an African one called Boa Constrictor (Orlick, 1978; Hatcher, Pape, & Nicosia, 1988). The child who is Dragon catches other children, who then hold hands with the Dragon. As groups of captured chil-

dren form, children can break off in pairs to form new Dragons. The last child to elude the Dragons becomes the new Dragon, and the game begins again.

Games such as this can stimulate children's understanding of number ideas, spatial concepts, music, cooperation, strategic planning, language, muscle control, science, and art, as well as social studies—what a great way to integrate learning! If children teach each other their family game favorites, or bring in a relative who can assist, so much the better.

For suggestions of many other games for this young age group, see also Kamii and DeVries (1980) and Sobel (1983). Often, little or no equipment is needed. Children might compile a book of rules for their games—invented or traditional—so everyone in the neighborhood learns how to share the fun.

Search yard sales, consignment shops, and neighborhood stores for board and card games, puzzles, maps, musical instruments, household objects, and other learning materials. Children can help make lotto games and puzzles, for example, from recycled products such as egg cartons, Styrofoam packing materials, pictures clipped from magazines and catalogs, or snapshots of the children in the group. Incorporate children's languages into the materials and directions. Children become eager assistants in putting together new activities for their classroom.

Many times, parents or local businesses willingly donate, or at least loan, diverse items such as jewelry, kitchen items, tools, mobility aids, or clothing. Collect chopsticks, kimonos, parkas, turbans, veils, moccasins, serapes, old cookie cutters, egg beaters, ice cream scoops, eyeglasses (with lenses removed), rolling pins, graters and grinders, pans, and a mortar and pestle—always making sure the items are appropriate for children's play based on the meaning of the item in the culture, and a variety of people and jobs are represented. Old and new toys—banks, vehicles, dolls—from many cultures appeal with certainty to all children.

Select activities wisely. Games rank among young children's favorite activities. Kamii and DeVries (1980, p. 3) offer three criteria for good group games. To be educationally useful, a group game should—

1. suggest something interesting and challenging for children to figure out how to do;

2. make it possible for children themselves to judge their success; and

3. permit all players to participate actively throughout the game.

These criteria—extensions of those already discussed—apply to nearly every other classroom activity as well.

Seek out a selection of games that can be played alone, some for one or two other children, and eventually a few for two or more teams, as children become more capable of following rules and cooperating with others. Urge children to improve their skills, and—instead of always cheering for a winner—focus on what it takes to be a productive team member.

Scoring? What better way for children to apply their early math skills than to

---

Games can stimulate children's understanding of number ideas, spatial concepts, music, cooperation, strategic planning, language, muscle control, science, and art, as well as social studies—what a great way to integrate learning!

---

keep track of their progress with stones, markers, hash marks, or even numbers. Choose games in which children throw one—and then two—dice to determine their move. Set up bowling with score sheets. The real need to list, count, add, or subtract is a great motivator for learning how to write children's names and numerals, and for figuring out how addition really works.

Puzzles in diverse classrooms portray a vast array of cultural groups, foods, transportation, homes, workplaces, and scenes that include those familiar to children in the group. Photo puzzles of children themselves, or wooden puzzles made by local crafters, are sure to captivate interest. Children can create their own puzzles, using their drawings, stories, or a collage of found objects such as leaves.

Unit blocks are probably the most valuable hands-on learning tool available because they contribute to virtually every area of an integrated, diverse curriculum (Figure 2). Unit blocks come in a variety of standard sizes that encourage children to experience math, social studies, physics, and a host of other encounters for themselves, alone or in concert with other children. The purchase of blocks is a lifetime investment; they appeal to children from toddlerhood through the elementary grades, so they're always in demand.

Children's learning through block play is also enhanced with a multitude of accessories, such as figures of people from various cultures and in many occupations, different types of vehicles including boats and trucks, wild and domestic animals, street signs, pulleys, and trees. Children can build many of their own block play props, write their own signs, and remember their bridges or cities or launch pads with drawings or photos that they make themselves.

By the early elementary years, most children are quite skilled at using blocks and accessories to construct fairly elaborate familiar or imagined structures. They can play board or running games. They

> ## To be educationally useful, a group game should—
>
> 1. suggest something interesting and challenging for children to figure out how to do;
> 2. make it possible for children themselves to judge their success;
> 3. permit all players to participate actively throughout the game (Kamii & DeVries, 1980, p. 3).

solve puzzles. All of these activities indicate their emerging ability to symbolize objects and ideas.

Promote mapping skills. Young children are just beginning to be able to grasp the idea that maps are symbols for representing much larger areas (Richards, 1976). During children's early years, maps are most meaningful when they are constructed by the children as miniatures of familiar environments—unit-block creations or floor-plan sketches of the classroom or home, streets from home to school, and other familiar routes, such as the way to a park or to their grandparent's house.

Field trips are a fine way to experience distance and space. To build on what the children are learning, tour the school building and grounds on the first day or two of school, walk around the neighborhood as the seasons change, visit construction sites to watch progress, and take a bus trip to a wharf or a farm. For more ideas on field trips as extended learning activities, see the last section of this chapter.

During their trips, children gain firsthand experience with directions, distance, space, and time. Afterward, they might recall landmarks and street names to list and then plot on a map. Maps can be drawn on the chalkboard or large sheets of paper, or even marked off with masking tape on the floor. Children can make

Figure 2. Potential Contributions of Blocks for Early Childhood Curriculum

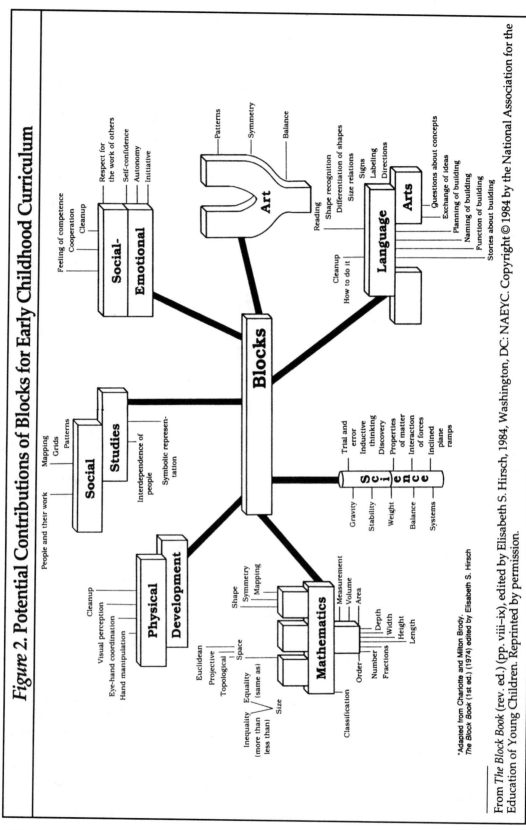

From *The Block Book* (rev. ed.) (pp. viii-ix), edited by Elisabeth S. Hirsch, 1984, Washington, DC: NAEYC. Copyright © 1984 by the National Association for the Education of Young Children. Reprinted by permission.

*Adapted from Charlotte and Milton Brody,
The Block Book (1st ed.) (1974) edited by Elisabeth S. Hirsch

buildings by cutting, pasting, and painting small boxes or milk cartons. How carefully skyscrapers must be balanced! Frozen ponds might be indicated with aluminum foil. Use recycled materials whenever possible for class projects.

State, U.S., or world maps may be posted in primary classrooms, of course, but they will be most valuable when accessible to children looking for familiar place names and tracing travel routes for families who moved within or immigrated to the United States. Although globes could be introduced as one of many mapping strategies with older primary children, even most adults have difficulty grasping the concepts of time and space that globes represent. Their practical use is limited until children have more experience with symbols. If possible, use world maps that are scale accurate, such as the Peters projection, rather than the traditional Mercator map that distorts the size of the Western continents.

Capitalize on the value of games and manipulatives. There is so much to be learned in hands-on, feet-on projects. As children work and play together, teachers are always nearby to ask thought-provoking questions, to guide and direct, to locate materials and resources, to respond to questions, and to encourage children's thinking about themselves and the world around them.

Adults' specific, seemingly casual comments about individual successes, such as "Nouke, how quickly you found your friends today when you played Hide and Seek! You must have been listening carefully," contribute far better to children's self-esteem and long-term development than the standard approach of awarding impersonal ribbons or certificates for achievements (Curry & Johnson, 1990).

When a positive atmosphere is established, children compliment each other on their progress and successes: "Yippee! You did that really hard puzzle all by yourself, Kevia!" Through experiences like these, children develop a positive, accurate picture of themselves as people, get to know other children as people who can succeed, and come to feel they are an integral part of an important group of friends.

At the same time, some common teaching materials and strategies can backfire, even when their intended use is to teach fairness and democracy. Games such as Old Maid, for example, stereotype and ridicule people, so they should be avoided. If children bring these types of games to school, discuss the materials, with sensitivity, as examples of subtle ways in which people feel hurt.

Selecting children for classroom responsibilities, for special tasks, for the order in which they receive their lunch, or as team members can be fraught with broken hearts. Find unbiased ways to select children for these activities, such as drawing names from a hat, so no child feels humiliated by being the last one chosen.

Above all, help children concentrate on the fun of participating and playing together, rather than on winning or completing the final product. In so doing we increase the probability that our long-term goals for children will be realized. The *process* of playing is exemplified by the many opportunities provided for young children to engage in dramatic play.

During children's early years, maps are most meaningful when they are constructed by the children as miniatures of familiar environments.

Dramatic play props

Through dramatic play, children try out different roles and behaviors in the security of their classroom. They can be anyone they choose. Children can experience what it is like to live in an igloo, to eat and drink while sitting on the floor, to wrap a flowing scarf around their waists, to walk with crutches.

The abundance of props for the dramatic play area can be rotated every week or two so that children's interest is always piqued by something new; but children should be able to count on a few permanent items, too. Make sure more than a single representative item is available for each group to avoid tokenism. Furniture, dolls and puppets, clothing, accessories, and tools from home and work—all culturally authentic—are the most common dramatic play items for young children. Label storage boxes so items can be retrieved easily.

Child-size furniture enables all children in the classroom to take charge of their environment, and to experience the past as well as the present and future. Move cradles and chairs about to create a bustling hospital on Angel Island, longhouses of the Iroquois, or trains carrying immigrants east and west. Include a rocking chair, a hammock, floor pillows, a futon, or other familiar furnishings that reflect the cultures of children and their surrounding community.

Dolls and puppets should represent many cultures, ages, abilities, and males and females, too. It's easy for manufacturers to add a tint to plastic dolls to create a range of skin tones, but look for dolls and

Help children concentrate on the fun of participating and playing together.

puppets with authentic facial features, hair, and clothing, as well as skin colors. Children can sew puppets, dolls, quilts, doll clothes, and other props with the help of an informed adult. Accurate illustrations in books can aid in the design.

Children always enjoy trying on dress-up clothing, whether it be a pair of tippy high heels or leather sandals, a briefcase or a brilliant sash. Seek clothing made by the group represented whenever possible; check with families and scout for finds at yard sales. Offer a balance of everyday, special occasion, contemporary, and historical clothing.

Housewares, tools, and workplace items help solidify children's understanding of the similarities that all human beings share. Select both historical and contemporary kitchen utensils (flour sifters, muffin tins, wok); foods (corn, rice, nuts, pasta, potatoes); items used in a variety of occupations (hard hats, fishing nets, spinning wheel, calculators, dictionaries in several languages); and other artifacts that children can use to extend their play and understanding of how people live and work.

Teachers are always nearby to ask thought-provoking questions, to guide and direct, to locate materials and resources, to respond to questions, and to encourage children's thinking about themselves and the world around them.

Bulletin boards

Bulletin boards and other school displays offer the most prominent and visible means for teachers to instill children's pride in their own efforts and their own heritages. The items displayed, therefore, should be primarily the results of children's own projects. Representative samples of all their work—writing, drawing, painting, sculpture, photos of them and their families at home and school, newspaper clippings they choose—can be hung for each other and visitors to see.

Encourage children to frame their works with larger sheets of construction paper, hang items at their own eye level, and work together to prepare pleasing exhibits. Children deserve options for their work:

- display it;
- file it away so they can measure their progress later in the year;
- take it home; or
- throw it away.

In classrooms where children know they can succeed, wastebaskets will be practically empty, and walls, filing cabinets, and the refrigerator at home will bulge.

Many teachers prefer to prepare occasional displays of their own, as well, to draw children's attention to something special. When buying or making these displays, avoid stereotyped materials,

> **Select historical and contemporary kitchen utensils, foods, items used in a variety of occupations, and other artifacts that children can use to extend their play and understanding of how people live and work.**

such as alphabet lists that illustrate the letter *I* with Indian or Igloo (neither is a long *I* sound anyway). Eliminate commercial and cartoon characters. Children see enough of them elsewhere. Instead, look for bright and beautiful colors and designs in Native American, Hispanic, African, and other art forms. Seek out posters in Spanish, Japanese, and other languages children speak with their families. Create collages from magazine and catalog pictures—including lots of faces and settings to demonstrate a wide range of diversity.

The fine arts

Along with literature (covered earlier in the children's books section), music and art are also fine arts. If children are to truly appreciate the diversity of human expression, they need familiarity with the variety of ways that cultures and individuals express beauty through their music and art, as through literature. When the three are combined, as they are in any well-integrated elementary curriculum, children are fascinated and eager to learn more.

Music. Music is one of the most valued expressions of cultural and personal identity. Music can bring tears to the eyes, laughter to the soul, and dancing to the feet. Nearly all young children love to sing, dance, listen to, and create their own music. Fortunately, recordings of hun-

Offer children options for their work:

- display it;
- file it away so they can measure their progress later in the year;
- take it home; or
- throw it away.

dreds of different musical sounds—harps, drums, bagpipes, triangles, solos, symphonies, voices, and instrumentals—are readily available. Eager-to-perform musicians reside in every community.

How many ways there are to bring children and music together! Children enjoy singing, playing, or dancing to recordings. They listen with rapt attention when older children or adults play for them. With some guidance, they can try simple instruments themselves or make their own musical instruments. Music, like story reading, should be a several-times-a-day occurrence in primary classrooms. Through music, children's senses are engaged as they remember, feel, imagine, move, play, and respond.

Through music, children's senses are engaged as they remember, feel, imagine, move, play, and respond.

The Americans All collection of *Music of America's Peoples* (Spottswood, 1989) inspires teachers to seek out other authentic ethnic musical expressions to share with children (some resources are listed in Part 3). Search for appealing music and recordings—old and new, classical, rock, folk, jazz, rap. Singing games and fingerplays—traditional and modern ones—are popular with young children, too. Some teachers strive to learn at least one new one each week.

Work with the school's music staff to enlarge the collection of real instruments available for children, and borrow them often so the children can strum, strike, shake, or blow with success. Invite older children to play familiar tunes for younger groups; after only a few lessons, fourth graders can play songs that are familiar and impressive to young ears. Collect diaphanous scarves,

---

The items displayed should be primarily the results of children's own projects.

---

clogging shoes, a tuxedo, and similar related items that can add to the fun of experiencing different styles of music.

Ask families and others in the community to share their favorite traditional songs, instruments, and singing games with the class, too. Families who may not be readers may well be musicians. Perhaps a parent, grandparent, or uncle could play some foot-stomping Appalachian fiddle and teach children some dance steps. Others might be willing to sing—in their home language—their child's favorite lullaby that has been passed down for generations. How easy it is for children to learn real, meaningful words in another language when they are sung to a beautiful melody.

Even music, however, sometimes can be counterproductive to our efforts to demonstrate respect for people. For example, a song such as "Ten Little Indians" (and the Indian headdresses often used with it) treat Native Americans as objects. Neither the music nor the costumes "reflect their diverse lifestyles, histories, work, music, or celebrations" (Ramsey, 1979, p. 28). Before sharing a song or dance with children, think critically about the message conveyed to assure that diversity is valued, that religious beliefs are respected, and that any cultural group would be delighted to be the subject. Music can bring such joy to our lives!

Art. Just as with music, children experience art forms in two ways: as observers and as participants. Both experiences are equally critical in a developmentally

Projects should be the children's creation from start to finish.

appropriate classroom. Children can be surrounded every day with various artistic expressions from their own and other cultures, such as paintings, sculptures, wall hangings, rugs, or mobiles. Change the collection frequently so children feel at home with a variety of aesthetically pleasing items, and choose several different items from each group.

Touch, smell, sight, and sound are as much a part of the artistic experience as they are every other area of learning. Find out what local clay, wool, flower petals, onion skins, or other folk art materials and styles might be brought into the classroom. Perhaps children could visit a potter at the potter's wheel, a glass blower, a weaver, or an ironsmith.

Ask families or other people in the area if they would share a treasured art object and explain to the children its significance. The simplest items, such as a soapstone Eskimo child and her dog or a set of Russian Matryoshka stacking dolls, may have the most appeal. Take a walking trip to a hands-on museum or sculpture garden. For more marvelous suggestions of ways to promote children's aesthetic development, indoors and out, see Feeney and Moravcik (1987).

As children become acquainted with many types of art, they will be curious to know how the effects were achieved and with what materials. For children to truly appreciate how art varies within and among cultures, a wealth of different natural media must be available for children to explore, from twigs and leaves to cotton and stones. Recyclable materials, such as buttons, yarn ends, ceramic tile pieces, upholstery scraps, and other similar items are usually had-for-the-asking in every community. Colors for children's selection must cover the spectrum from black and brown to white and everything in between, and with all being seen as equally valuable.

Demonstrate and explain artistic techniques so that children can experiment with their own interpretations—a teaching process illuminated by elementary art teacher Jo Miles Schuman:

> It is not expected that students will be able to create pieces of art as fine as the examples shown them, which are usually the result of years of training and tradition. But when they work with materials with their own hands, students appreciate the skills of those artisans even more. At the same time, they enjoy the creative process themselves and gain some confidence in their own abilities. Exposing students to art from all over the world brings them the wonder of art in all its many forms, expands their knowledge of what art is, and shows them the variety of ways design problems can be solved. (1981, p. ix)

The criteria set forth earlier for learning materials and activities apply to art as well as to all other classroom endeavors: Projects should be the children's creation

Identify local resources of interest to children. Ask for recommendations. Look for the unusual!

from start to finish. Copying mundane crafts, cutting and pasting worksheets, or coloring in someone else's drawing is neither art nor of much value for learning (Jefferson, 1963).

Guests and field trips

Every community has historical markers, museums, restored buildings, residents who remember the olden days, advocates for people with varying abilities, cultural centers, or groups who recognize the finest talents in the area. Whether guests are invited to the school or children take an excursion, a great deal of planning—always with the children's fullest possible participation—is involved. Both types of activities contribute further to an educational environment that promotes children's awareness of the world around them.

The first task is to identify local resources of interest to children. Ask children, their families, colleagues, and librarians for recommendations, even if the community is a familiar one. Look for the unusual! For example, a Tenement Museum on New York's Lower East Side is the only museum to honor the homes of urban pioneers. Track down local legends or true stories, such as the one about heroine Kate Shelley who saved a train from plunging off a bridge into a rain-swollen Iowa river. Seek out living history museums or farms, working farms or archaeological digs, and cemeteries in which to do grave rubbings of names that reflect families' origins.

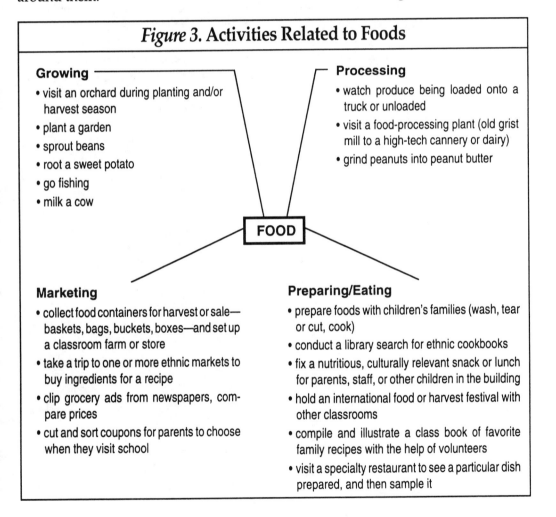

Figure 3. Activities Related to Foods

Growing
- visit an orchard during planting and/or harvest season
- plant a garden
- sprout beans
- root a sweet potato
- go fishing
- milk a cow

Processing
- watch produce being loaded onto a truck or unloaded
- visit a food-processing plant (old grist mill to a high-tech cannery or dairy)
- grind peanuts into peanut butter

FOOD

Marketing
- collect food containers for harvest or sale—baskets, bags, buckets, boxes—and set up a classroom farm or store
- take a trip to one or more ethnic markets to buy ingredients for a recipe
- clip grocery ads from newspapers, compare prices
- cut and sort coupons for parents to choose when they visit school

Preparing/Eating
- prepare foods with children's families (wash, tear or cut, cook)
- conduct a library search for ethnic cookbooks
- fix a nutritious, culturally relevant snack or lunch for parents, staff, or other children in the building
- hold an international food or harvest festival with other classrooms
- compile and illustrate a class book of favorite family recipes with the help of volunteers
- visit a specialty restaurant to see a particular dish prepared, and then sample it

Make sure speakers or tour guides understand how children learn best: hands-on, involving, authentic experiences.

As themes for children's in-depth study evolve throughout the year, children can vote to select the types of special activities that most interest them. See Figure 3 for a web of just a few of the possible guest and field trip ideas related to foods.

Whenever other adults are involved in a class project, orient them to the group's goals and interests before they meet the children. Make sure the speakers or tour guides understand how children learn best—hands-on, involving, authentic experiences rather than just lecturing. Strive to include as many as possible of children's five senses in every activity.

Sometimes a field trip is necessary to give children the background experiences necessary for them to better comprehend the topic. Many of today's children, for example, are unaware of where milk comes from, the different materials used to construct a home, or the steps involved in sewing a garment. The early childhood years used to be a time when children in every culture learned these types of things at their families' knees. Our task is to give children real experiences that undergird not only their appreciation of similarities and differences among cultures and individuals but all of their future learning.

Every teacher can structure the classroom environment to expose children to the wealth of variety in people and the artifacts of their cultures. This backdrop is but only the beginning of our efforts to ensure that children acquire the skills, attitudes, and knowledge they need to live and work in a diverse world. *How* children learn is just as important as *what* they learn about themselves and each other. Part 2 turns our attention to how to integrate curriculum materials into the substance, as well as the style, of teaching children to value diversity.

Integrating Diversity Into the Curriculum

You teach best what you most need to learn.
—Richard Bach

Appropriate learning materials for older children recount portions of the history of many of the peoples who live in North America. More mature children are developing a firmer grasp of the passage of time, and their more refined cognitive abilities enable them to deal with more abstract ideas. They can also benefit from meaningful, diverse experiences such as those recommended here.

But young children, as we have seen, must have a variety of experiences about life *now* before history can begin to make sense. They must first get to know themselves—along with their families, friends in school, their neighbors, and people they will play with and work alongside all their lives.

Primary teachers who embed respect and success within the daily fabric of their classrooms celebrate contemporary similarities and differences, and unfold children's awareness of their own— and their friends'—personal histories and interests. Family members become active participants in their children's education, at home and at school. In the process, children begin to recognize the common threads that unite us all as Americans.

Learning that values diversity takes place naturally—in everyday classroom events and activities that relate to children's lives at home and at play—and thus makes sense to children. Children improve their handwriting skills by penning their own family stories, for example. They learn how mathematics works by keeping score when they play traditional games, or by measuring when they cook or construct replicas of their neighborhoods. Reading and language are perfect for learning more about each other as children share their original books, hear fascinating stories that span generations, note the similarity of expressions from one language to

Teachers who embed respect and success within the fabric of their classrooms celebrate contemporary similarities and differences.

another, and pretend to play the roles of people today and yesterday.

Although world history is not taught per se in the primary grades, it is important for teachers of young children to understand the events and circumstances involving cultural groups—ranging from the first Americans to the most recent of immigrants. This balanced knowledge enables teachers to select authentic materials and to implement teaching strategies that convey respect for children's families and their cultures. Curiosity is contagious, so teachers who establish an atmosphere of eagerness to learn are sure to pass on their quest for knowledge.

Part 2 begins by reviewing four intertwined teaching strategies that are the heart of a developmentally appropriate, diverse curriculum:

- democratic conflict resolution,
- positive discipline,
- antibias advocacy, and
- cooperative learning.

As children experience genuine pride in themselves and others, learn greater self-control, solve real problems, grow in wisdom with each other, see their families involved in their education, and sense they are an important part of their communities, they increasingly become successful learners. They become committed to democracy, truth, fairness, and the other ideals shared by all Americans. These children are readers and writers. They are mathematicians. They are scientists. Musicians. Artists. And anthropologists. Poets. Decision makers. They are learning what they need to know now—and for their future continued success.

Chapter 6 suggests a few lively diversity activities easily integrated as a part of the primary curriculum, and includes ideas for using a variety of resources. More specific learning activities building on the Americans All program are found elsewhere (McCracken, 1992). Children's study of themselves and others can truly be an exciting adventure. Teachers—along with children's families and the entire community—can lead the way to fuller lives and a more harmonious world by incorporating diversity into children's everyday experiences.

Chapter 5

Teaching Strategies

Before choosing exactly HOW and WHAT children are going to learn, teachers find out WHO the children are. Observations of and conversations with children, their families, and other professionals provide the chief sources of information about each child's skills, languages, values, and interests. Throughout the year, children's strengths and weaknesses as individuals and as a class continue to be identified.

Based on the information that accumulates every day, teachers tailor—minute by minute—a primary program to fit each child, the group, and the community. Why? Because

> It is the responsibility of the educational system to adjust to the developmental needs and levels of the children it serves; children should not be expected to adapt to an inappropriate system. (Bredekamp, 1987, p. 13)

Many of today's children enter school with backgrounds in Head Start or other early childhood programs already rich in diversity and developmentally appropriate learning opportunities (Head Start Bureau, 1992; McCracken, in press). Many children live in ethnically blended families or neighborhoods. Today's communities are diverse in many ways. Television has opened other human relations vistas, sometimes woefully inaccurate.

The experiences and composition of each class give direction to how children learn to appreciate themselves and each other (Table 6). A supportive classroom atmosphere is far more effective than an isolated activity or two to boost children's self-esteem or to celebrate a holiday. Therefore, these recommendations apply to a *daily style of professional practice* that is naturally infused with content that values human diversity and democracy. This style of teaching addresses all areas of children's development, and gives students ample opportunities to succeed.

Few children have extensive positive experiences with racially, culturally, economically, or otherwise different children. At the beginning of the school term or whenever a new child is enrolled, the children will thus benefit if their interest in each other's physical differences and similarities is acknowledged. Young children readily become comfortable with various skin colors, hair textures, facial features, languages, abilities, and other human features when their classroom is filled with trust and respect.

Table 6. The Approach Depends Upon the Class Composition

- If your class is already diverse, then learning about themselves will simultaneously provide learning about diversity.

- If your class is all children of color, the first task is fostering positive personal and group identity in the face of negative messages of racism. Further tasks include learning about the diversity within the class and then about groups not present.

- If your class is all European American, developing children's positive personal and group identity must include learning to appreciate and accept the differences among themselves. Introducing activities about ethnic/cultural diversity not present in the class should be done in conjunction with countering socially prevailing stereotypes and biases about people with color. Begin with a group that has some visibility in the children's world because they live in the larger community or are represented on TV programs the children watch.

From *Anti-Bias Curriculum: Tools for Empowering Young Children* (p. 37) by L. Derman-Sparks & the A.B.C. Task Force, 1989, Washington, DC: NAEYC. Copyright © 1989 by Louise Derman-Sparks. Table revised 1993 by L. Derman-Sparks and printed by permission.

Children are curious and may ask potentially embarrassing questions about appearance, such as "Why is Jamal's skin so dark?" Appropriate responses briefly and honestly address the real questions *and* are sensitive to children's feelings:

> "Jamal's skin is dark brown because his mom and dad have dark brown skin. We all have a special chemical in our skin called melanin. If you have a lot of melanin, your skin is dark. If you only have a little, your skin is light. How much melanin you have in your skin depends on how much your birth parents have in theirs." (Derman-Sparks, Gutiérrez, & Phillips, 1989, p. 5)

Language can also be a source of children's concern, as indicated by questions such as "Why does Miyoko speak funny?" An appropriate response to a question about language might be

> "Miyoko speaks *differently* than you do. She speaks Japanese because that's what her mom and dad speak. You speak English like your mom and dad. It is okay to ask questions about what Miyoko is saying, but it is *not* okay to say that her speech sounds funny because that can

hurt her feelings." (Derman-Sparks, Gutiérrez, & Phillips, 1989, p. 5)

After children have satisfied their basic curiosity about easily observable differences, they are ready to get to know each other as human beings with similar feelings, families, needs, and dreams.

The proven teaching strategies reviewed here meet the criteria established earlier for learning materials and activities. They promote children's various intelligences. These techniques lead to achievement of positive long-range goals for children. Most of these strategies are already in place in professional-practice classrooms. The practical application of strategies in an integrated, diverse curriculum is the center of attention here.

The composition of each year's class largely determines the direction of how children learn to value diversity.

Pride and self-esteem

Individuals and groups within every culture are proud of themselves for many reasons, as examined earlier in Commitment #3. Teaching techniques designed to promote self-esteem, therefore, are shaped to fit children's personal/cultural styles and values (Hale, 1991). Sound teaching strategies contribute to children's feelings of pride and unity—never superiority or divisiveness—in themselves and other people.

Sensitive teachers are acutely aware that children's diversity is ever present in classrooms. Adopted children, children with interracial heritages, children who live in blended families, and children who are growing up in many other circumstances in our country all deserve support for their individual and group identities (Wardle, 1987, 1990a, 1992b; Hearst, 1993).

If there are Native American children, for instance, teachers are led by the knowledge that many Native American families

- respect and value the dignity of the individual;

- focus on cooperation;

- value sharing;

- see time as a continuum, with no beginning and no end (not clock watchers); and

- listen to wisdom of their elders but also learn to be independent, and to live by and learn from the decisions they make (Foerster & Little Soldier, 1978).

For each child's culture, teachers identify the components of what the child's family considers to be *authentic* self-esteem. Informal conversations with families help pinpoint goals for children. Encourage these attributes with children in school. Why? Because "encouragement . . . fosters autonomy, positive self-esteem, a willingness to explore and an acceptance of self and others," (Hitz & Driscoll, 1988, p. 13).

Ways to encourage children. Many well-intentioned adults contend that praise and rewards are the best ways to promote children's development and self-esteem. But the evidence is otherwise: "The long-range effect of encouragement is self-confidence. The long-range effect of praise is dependence on others" (Nelsen, 1987, p. 103).

Reviews of research (Gottfried, 1983; Cannella, 1986; Curry & Johnson, 1990; Kohn, 1991) and popular articles, alike (Maynard, 1989), consistently reveal that empty and excessive praise, lavish distri-

> # Appropriate teaching strategies contribute to children's feelings of pride and unity—never superiority or divisiveness—in themselves and other people.

bution of stickers, and similarly trite social or tangible rewards

- erode children's *genuine* sense of self-esteem;

- undermine children's intrinsic motivation and self-control;

- infer that the activity has no worth in its own right;

- reduce children's persistence;

- lead children to take on the easiest tasks;

- discourage children's creativity; and

- foster children's dependence, rather than autonomy.

How then are children *encouraged* in developmentally appropriate ways? Teachers who encourage children

- give specific, effective praise (without setting children up for failure) such as "How carefully you are writing the letters in your name, Khamsay";

- privately initiate encouragement (rather than publicly comparing children or urging competition), such as sitting down by a child at a learning center and commenting, "That new geometric puzzle certainly captivated you! You've been working diligently on it for half an hour";

- help children appreciate their improvements in behavior or in mastering a process (rather than evaluating a finished product), such as stating, "You figured out how to smooth the papier maché with your hand to make the plateau level"; and

- offer sincere, direct comments in a natural voice, such as saying, "You can be proud of the way you used your words to negotiate for your turn on the swing" (based on Hitz & Driscoll, 1988).

Fostering self-esteem through language development. Children come to school with a wide variety of language experiences. Some may already be reading; some can write their own names; others are skilled listeners or storytellers. Teachers of young children enjoy the privilege of expanding children's literacy in many directions, both written and oral. Every activity suggested in this guide promotes children's language development, so the topic emphasized in this section is how to foster self-esteem in children for whom English is a second language.

Although English is the official language of the United States, many people are fluent in other languages as well. In a democracy such as ours, families rightfully choose the language they wish to use to communicate with their children. The school's respect for families' culture and language is essential, then, for children to feel pride in themselves and in their heritage.

For each child and each family's culture, seek to identify the components of *authentic* self-esteem.

> ## Teachers who encourage children
>
> - give specific, effective praise;
> - privately initiate encouragement;
> - help children appreciate their improvements in behavior or in mastering a process; and
> - offer sincere, direct comments in a natural voice (based on Hitz & Driscoll, 1988).

At the same time, teachers help parents to prepare children to succeed in the broader society. Citizens in most industrialized nations are bilingual. The recent influx of immigrants challenges our schools to keep up with our multicultural populations. At one elementary school in Brooklyn, children speak 26 languages, from Armenian to Urdu, and more than 150 languages are now spoken in America (Leslie, 1991).

Working with young children and their families, many of whom speak little if any English, requires flexibility, sensitivity, and a wealth of accurate information about how children acquire language. It is imperative that children maintain their positive self-esteem while they gradually learn a second (or third) language and culture in school (NAEYC & NAECS/SDE, 1991).

Some specific strategies for building children's pride through bilingualism are offered in Table 7. For further details on working with non–English-speaking children, see Williams and De Gaetano (1985), Schiller and Bermudez (1988), Soto (1991), Wong Fillmore (1991b), and McCracken (in press). Communication with children and their families is greatly facilitated, of course, when teachers themselves use the community's languages with ease and grace.

Table 7. Building Pride in Bilingualism

The possibilities are endless for teachers of young children who, as role models, are in a unique position to establish the tone, or "classroom climate," through decision making, collaboration, interactions, and activities.

Teachers of young children are currently implementing a variety of educationally sound strategies. In addition, based upon the recent research, and what we know about young children, we can:

1. Accept individual differences with regard to language-learning time frames. It's a myth to think that young children can learn a language quickly and easily. . . .

2. Accept children's attempts to communicate, because trial and error are a part of the second language learning process. Negotiating meaning, and collaboration in conversations, is important. . . . Plan and incorporate opportunities for conversation such as dramatic play, storytime, puppetry, peer interactions, social experiences, field trips, cooking and other enriching activities.

3. Maintain an additive philosophy by recognizing that children need to acquire new language skills instead of replacing existing linguistic skills . . . .

4. Provide a stimulating, active, diverse linguistic environment with many opportunities for language use in meaningful social interactions. Avoid rigid or didactic grammatical approaches with young children . . . .

5. Incorporate culturally responsive experiences for all children. . . .

6. Use informal observations to guide the planning of activities, interactions, and conversations for speakers of other languages.

7. Provide an *accepting* classroom climate that values culturally and linguistically diverse young children . . . .

From "Research in Review. Understanding Bilingual/Bicultural Young Children" by L. D. Soto, January 1991, *Young Children*, 46(2), pp. 34–35. Copyright © 1991 by the National Association for the Education of Young Children. Reprinted by permission.

Practical ways to promote pride. A developmentally appropriate, diverse curriculum enhances children's self-esteem. An atmosphere of trust, respect, and responsibility promotes children's genuine pride in themselves as successful learners and friends.

Names—of individuals, activities, and groups—are a prominent indicator of attitudes about self and others. On the first day of school, or when new children enroll, children feel honored to tell teachers and friends what they prefer to be called (see Individual activities, p. 84, Chapter 6). Address children and family members in a manner consistent with the traditions of their cultures (Morrow, 1989). Spell and pronounce children's names carefully in accordance with cultural and personal preferences.

Respect for each family's culture and language is essential for children to feel pride in themselves and in their heritage.

Names crop up in other ways during the school day as well. When teachers call children to sit on a carpet to hear a story, they can ask children to sit like pretzels or in tailor style, instead of like Indians (few Native Americans ever sat that way). The terminology used to describe groups changes as attempts are made to be both accurate and positive in referring to the indigenous and immigrant peoples, as well as many others who share common attributes. Help children recognize contemporary usage; explain why older books use other names to refer to Native Americans, African Americans, European Americans, or Mexican Americans, and why the names may well change again as we develop more sensitivity to people.

Earlier we discussed how important it is to choose members of committees or teams in fair and varied ways. Children quickly pick up on what the assigned names of ability groups, such as those for reading, really mean. The best professional practice minimizes the use of homogeneous groupings, and strives to give children opportunities to learn at their own rates and in their own styles—and from each other—in heterogeneous groups (Bredekamp, 1987; NAESP, 1990). Whenever small, flexible groups are used, children could vote to select a name in which they feel pride. They may change it whenever they agree to do so.

Democracy and cooperation are among the shared American values practiced daily in classrooms structured for success. Young children are very willing and able to accept real responsibility for themselves and others (Guideline #2 in Chapter 3). Teachers involve children in every task. With a bit of preparation on how to handle the job, children can recycle paper in a handy box, read stories to younger children, assist the librarian, safely keep the playground clean, and engage in a host of other collaborative tasks.

Genuine pride is enhanced by trust, respect, and responsibility.

Children savor the results of, and readily evaluate, their own valuable efforts. Their *real* achievements at *real* tasks surely promote their self-worth. Children select which pieces of their own artwork to exhibit. They choose which of their original poems to display. They choose whether to take a photo or draw a picture of an intricate model they constructed of their apartment building.

When children routinely make real-life choices such as these, they learn to evaluate their own efforts, to trust their own judgment, and to experience the logical results of their decisions—they are becoming autonomous! When children feel proud of and responsible for themselves, they are far more likely to be in control of themselves.

Self-discipline

Young children who make lots of noise, hit each other, wander around, fail to pay attention, or otherwise disrupt their own learning as well as the education of other children are often either

- overwhelmed by physical or emotional factors (such as hunger, inadequate care, or lack of security), or
- bored (perhaps the work is too simple, unrelated to their lives, or far beyond their developmental capacity) (Greenberg, 1988).

On the other hand, when children know that school is a welcoming place, when

Children learn at their own rates and in their own styles, as well as from each other.

they decide about things that affect them, and when they tackle meaningful challenges, their self-control is promoted. A diverse classroom creates a setting in which children can be reasonably well behaved and intensely involved in the pursuit of knowledge.

The most difficult learning challenges of the early years are for children to get along with each other, to solve problems with words instead of fists or feet, and to cooperate with a variety of people.

Positive, future-oriented approaches to helping children learn self-discipline place the responsibility for proper behavior on the *children* (Smith & Davis, 1976; Shure & Spivack, 1978; Stone, 1978; Miller, 1984; NAEYC, 1986; Honig, 1987; Nelsen, 1987). Never place control in the hands of a threatening, vindictive adult (Smith & Davis, 1976; Gartrell, 1987). These time-tested approaches begin with prevention.

Prevention. What are primary children expected to learn in a diverse classroom with regard to their behavior? The goals for any appropriate program for children stress that children are expected to be fair and friendly, responsible decision makers, cooperative, proud of themselves, and thus growing toward greater self-control. Children achieve none of these goals if their behavior is controlled through fear, humiliation, or bribes (Greenberg, 1992).

In schools that promote democracy and responsibility, problems are prevented whenever possible. Teachers create a friendly, respectful classroom climate that

Real achievements at *real* tasks promote self-worth.

invites children to learn together. Children are held responsible for their own actions.

Each fall, children and teachers work out their own class rules to help children do their best at school. Children who attended good preschool programs likely have experience with this process. Teachers guide discussions so they are short and focused, but carried out in the spirit of democratic problem solving (for details, see Democratic conflict resolution, p. 58, this chapter). With help, children identify critical areas in which rules are needed—usually safety, fairness, or conflict resolution. Children think through the reasons for their rules.

After the basics are determined, urge children to express a few general rules in terms of what they are expected *to do*. These are examples of positive rules primary children might set for themselves:

- We use our words to solve problems fairly.
- We respect each other's bodies and feelings.
- We walk quietly in the hallway.

Children are still learning to control themselves, so they won't follow their rules 100% of the time. The strategy is prevention. Teachers can help children recognize, in advance, *natural, logical* consequences of breaking their rules: Mean children have no friends; careless children clean up their own messes.

When children anticipate real consequences such as these, the need for artificial consequences diminishes considerably. Nelsen wisely recommends that any established, immediate consequences fit these three criteria: "related, respectful," *and* "rea-

In a diverse classroom, children are reasonably well behaved and intensely involved in the pursuit of knowledge.

sonable" (1987, p. 73). All three are essential for the consequences to effectively help children achieve self-discipline, and thus to prevent many difficulties. A 3-Rs consequence might be that the child who spills glue on the floor is expected to clean it up; an artificial consequence might be the loss of recess or banishment to the time-out chair. Artificial consequences are, in reality, merely punishments.

Punishments are likely to backfire. Research on the short- and long-range effects of this popular childrearing strategy has conclusively shown that "children who are punished feel humiliated . . . hide their mistakes . . . tend to be angry and aggressive . . . and fail to develop control of themselves" (NAEYC, 1986, p. 9). Other consequences of punishment are resentment, revenge, and rebellion (Nelsen, 1987).

Therefore, blaming, forced apologies, name calling, shaming, lectures, bribes, fear, and other punitive approaches have absolutely no place in a professional-practice classroom. Punishment fails to pave the way to success and self-esteem.

Rather, professionals should inspire children to take increasing control of their own behavior. Young children go to great lengths to please adults and to get along with each other. They are eager to learn. Adults impart the social and thinking skills children need to succeed, today and tomorrow.

Democratic conflict resolution. We grown-ups are always trying to gain greater control of our behavior—whether it's our eating habits, our anger, or our tendency to procrastinate. Children, with far less experience, are also trying to better control themselves. They pick up their cues about how to behave by watching and listening to people around them. "Please," "Thank you," and "Excuse me" are how friends act toward each other.

More than a few self-imposed cultural rules and good examples

Self-disciplined people are adept at making decisions about how to behave.

are needed to instill self-control. Skills are essential. Self-disciplined people are adept at making decisions about how to behave. Sometimes our choices of behavior are suitable; other times they disappoint. Children experience true cause-and-effect when they watch what is happening, generate possible solutions to the problem, choose a possible resolution, take action, and then live with the consequences (Shure & Spivack, 1978).

Conversely, if adults always impose their ideas of how to overcome a difficulty, children are robbed of valuable opportunities to learn to solve their own problems. They'll always rely on someone else to figure a way out for them. Similarly, if adults set standard punishments for breaking the rules, children never experience what it is like to live with the *real* consequences of their own decisions.

Children become truly self-disciplined by becoming skilled decision makers. Therefore, adults teach children the steps involved in the process of democratic conflict resolution. Children apply this process—sometimes called "using your words"—whenever they have a disagreement (Table 8). At first, adults guide children through the four simple steps. Soon, children solve their problems on their own. It's so sensible and so effective that adults use the technique, too!

Let's see how this strategy works. Watch these first graders, who learned how to

Professionals inspire children to take increasing control of their own behavior.

Table 8. Democratic Conflict Resolution

Step	Action
1. "Tell us what happened."	Allow each child to explain the problem.
2. Summarize.	Summarize what they say. Include each child's point of view.
3. "What could you do about this problem?"	Ask children for possible solutions. Consider all possibilities. You may say, "I wonder if there is another way to handle this problem," but don't suggest any solution.
4. Help the children choose a solution.	Do not give any hint of what you think they should do—it is their decision.

From *Helping Children Love Themselves and Others* (p. 26) by J.B. McCracken (Ed.), 1990, Washington, DC: Children's Foundation. Copyright © 1990 by The Children's Foundation. Reprinted by permission.

use their words in preschool, go through the four problem-solving steps and use their own good judgment.

> Sadhana is using the giant magnifier to look at a variety of weavings, including some the children in the group have made themselves. Tomislav would like a turn.
>
> "Sadhana, can I please look through the magnifying glass?"
>
> She replies, "I'm not finished yet."
>
> "But you've been looking for a long time. I already read a book, waiting for you to finish," Tomislav points out. (The children explain the problem through natural conversation.) "I'm tired of waiting." (Tomislav summarizes the problem.)
>
> (Now come the solutions.)
>
> Sadhana clearly is not willing to stop instantly, as she retorts, "Well, you'll just have to wait longer."
>
> Tomislav is not about to give up so easily. "How long will it be until you're done, then?" he asks.
>
> Sadhana replies in a friendly tone, "Oh, about two minutes."
>
> Tomislav is delighted. "Super!"
>
> (The children choose their own solution.)
>
> "I'll come get you when I'm done," she offers.

Contrast this to a scenario of two children tugging on the magnifier and breaking off one of its legs, whines of "Teacher, she won't let me have a turn!", and—in the ultimate robbery of learning opportunities—an adult who proclaims, "We'll just have to put the magnifier away until you can quit fighting."

Children learn to talk their way through far more heated arguments than this. They can resolve differences—democratically and fairly—among themselves on issues large and small. They even recommend it to others: After hearing early news about the fighting in the 1991 Gulf War, a four-year-old who practices conflict resolution at home and school remarked, "They should have used their words!"

Sometimes, though, the dilemma seems too difficult or children can't come to agreeable terms. What then? Class meetings are an ideal method for democratically dealing with everyday decisions as well as thorny issues (Nelsen, 1987). As described by Nelsen, class meetings have four purposes:

1. to give compliments,
2. to help each other,
3. to solve problems, and
4. to plan events (Nelsen, 1987, p. 117).

These meetings are daily events in which children set the agenda, listen to each other, think through their options, and

Keep in mind what we *really* want children to learn.

vote on what to do. This democratic, respectful process fits within developmentally appropriate program goals, and is certainly workable in primary classrooms. Parents can implement it with equal success in family meetings at home. Through democratic problem-solving processes such as these, children learn to make and trust their own decisions.

Skeptics about this style of instilling self-discipline might find it helpful to focus on what we *really* want children—both those involved and any bystanders—to learn through every experience. This reasonable, future-oriented style of self-discipline—that promotes responsibility and wise decision making—becomes the clear choice!

Problem solving

The same thinking skills used in the democratic conflict resolution process apply to every other real-life encounter as well. Scientists, historians, physicians, mathematicians, computer programmers, educators—all use these same strategies every day: *identify* problems, *gather* details, *observe* data, *analyze* information, and *draw* conclusions (Seefeldt, 1975; Holt, 1989).

Why offer children ditto sheets with silly imaginary problems when pressing, riveting issues face our nation and world? Although these topics aren't neatly fragmented into math or spelling packages, they encompass many areas of the curriculum and give children useful ways to apply their emerging skills, thereby fostering self-confidence and competence. These results are far more satisfying and of greater service to humanity than any test score!

Consider how concern for the environment and the study of local native peoples overlap for young elementary children in the Bronx who start the year by exploring the local surroundings to find parts of the environment that would have been there when the Indians inhabited the region, such as trees, animals and the Hudson River. Soon they are gathering mature ears of corn from plants started by the third grade the preceding spring. This corn, which is supplemented by store-bought corn, is dried, separated from the cob, pounded in a hollow log and stored for the May feast. Before the feast is held in the warming days of spring, sugar maple sap will be collected from trees using taps and buckets and the sap will be boiled down to syrup. (Caduto & Bruchac, 1988, p. 6)

Respect for children's cultures is embedded within appropriate experiences such as these when children use numbers, read and write, and explore science and social studies to solve real problems. Objects from *many* cultures float or sink just as well as those that represent only one or two different backgrounds (families and teachers simply carefully select objects that can be plunged into water by curious children). Children locate various building materials when studying shelters past and present. They figure out the effects of weather on how people dress (clothing styles and fabrics); what crops are grown for food, clothing, or shelter; and how housing is designed and built (stone, steep roofs, portable).

What real problems can children identify with an adult's guidance? Let's take just one example of a seemingly frivolous problem.

Perhaps all the children are talking about a rap group star puppet they've seen advertised on TV. Think of the multicultural- and consumer-education possibilities posed by this "problem"! First, children figure out how much money they need, and how to raise money to buy the puppet. Suppose they decide to have an international art show. Committees are needed for publicity, displays, pricing, tickets, cashiers, refreshments.

After the event, with money in hand, children can compare puppet prices. (It's off to the school library to look up stores' telephone numbers or newspaper ads.)

Children vote on which store will get their business, then arrange for a shopping trip to purchase the item.

Next comes product evaluation. Is the puppet's performance equal to that portrayed in the ad? Is it sturdy or fragile? Does it seem as big in real life? Is the rap star fairly represented? Do other children, the manufacturer, store owner, and TV station need to know the findings? Children can write letters and newsletter articles: Is the rap puppet a good gift choice? Why or why not?

The most valuable lessons in language arts, math, science, and problem solving are found in the everyday world—and children are self-motivated when learning takes place in the context of what is important to them! Children identify serious issues that appeal to their developing sense of responsibility, such as the effects of pollution, how to meaningfully celebrate any holiday (Neugebauer, 1990; Wardle, 1990), ways to deal with discrimination, and efforts to assist homeless people. One first grade class chose, for instance, to decorate lunch bags and collect nails and other building supplies for Habitat for Humanity. Now these children can walk or drive past the finished home and know that their contributions made a difference for people in their neighborhood.

Opportunities to solve *real, important* dilemmas abound in every classroom and community. Adult leadership helps children observe, identify issues, collect information, analyze data, agree on actions to take, and stand up for what's fair and right. See Table 9 for further suggestions on how to begin to apply all-American activist skills in classrooms.

Activities that involve food are always popular and lend themselves well to multi-intelligence learning. Take baking bread! Children apply problem-solving and communication skills to select a recipe from one culture, locate ingredients, read directions, measure, mix, set the oven temperature, shape the dough, bake for a specified time, watch changes that take place, store loaves safely, dis-

Why offer ditto sheets with imaginary problems when pressing, riveting issues face children every day?

Table 9. Activism Activities

- Be alert for unfair practices in your school or neighborhood that directly affect your children's lives. You may be the first to identify the problem, or the children may bring a problem to your attention.

- Consider the interests and dynamics of your group of children. Do they care about the problem? What kind of actions would work with them?

- Consider your comfort. Is the issue one you feel comfortable addressing? What strategies do you prefer?

- Consider the parents' comfort. Do you want their agreement beforehand? Do you just plan to inform them of your plans? Do you want to include them in the activity?

- Try out the activity. If it works, great! If it doesn't, try again with a different activity!

From *Anti-Bias Curriculum: Tools for Empowering Young Children* (p. 83) by L. Derman-Sparks & the A.B.C. Task Force, 1989, Washington, DC: NAEYC. Copyright © 1989 by Louise Derman-Sparks. Reprinted by permission.

Children are self-motivated when learning is in the context of what is important to them!

- enabling children to enjoy working together, and

- encouraging children to develop their seven intelligences in the process.

play them attractively, and enjoy the fruits of their labors. Math, science, and reading are all kneaded!

Food is also a precious resource, so in a classroom that respects children, food is for eating (Holt, 1989). Other art materials abound—recycled paper and fabric scraps, boxes, packing supplies—so there is no reason to use rice instead of sand or wood shavings in a sand table, or macaroni instead of wooden beads for painting or stringing. *Eating* food is just one more way children work together to be part of solutions to complicated dilemmas.

With every project, teacher and children evaluate the activity to determine learnings: What did they accomplish? What would they do differently next time? What techniques were most effective? Why? How could they follow through in the future?

Wise teachers structure the environment to assure that children work in pairs, on teams, and in committees to accomplish real tasks, large and small. When one child's aunt arrives with a tape to teach everyone a dance she learned as a child in Puerto Rico, children move the tables and desks out of the way. One child sets up the tape player. Children find their own partners. Perhaps a child who is skilled at dance takes the hand of a child who has less experience, and soon both are happily responding to the music.

Wise teachers structure the environment to assure that children work in pairs, on teams, and in committees to accomplish real tasks.

Cooperative learning

A carefully structured cooperative environment that offers challenging learning tasks, that allows students to make key decisions about how they perform those tasks, and that emphasizes the value (and skills) of helping each other to learn constitutes an alternative to extrinsic motivators, an alternative both more effective over the long haul and more consistent with the ideals of educators. (Kohn, 1991, p. 86)

In other words, cooperative learning *isn't* taking place if children are bribed to work together by offering pizza parties or computer certificates (Slavin, 1991). Cooperative learning *is*

- building on children's growing awareness of people's diversity,

Social skills are polished. We have already seen how games, some computer programs, blocks, dramatic play props, music, and many other learning materials and activities inherently promote cooperation and learning. Children who work well together are far more likely to succeed in school and out.

Teachers create a basically cooperative (rather than highly competitive) classroom spirit when children are praised in encouraging ways:

Responses that promote cooperation

"Ari, you comforted Louisa with your hug."

"Let's put all the toys away."

"Look at the many shades of red Kim mixed with the paints."

"Maria, you were so thoughtful to help Ted pick up his crutches."

Responses that promote competition

"Ari, you're such a wonderful person."

"Who can put the most toys back on the shelf?"

"Kim is a great painter. I really like what you did."

"Maria, you are the best helper I know!"

(McCracken, 1990, p. 25)

Many of the examples throughout this guide demonstrate how small groups of children plan and carry out specific projects within a teacher's wise framework and with initial guidance about what is expected to be achieved and how to work together. Given these parameters, young children determine their partners or the structure and direction of their committees. They accommodate each other's diverse languages, learning modes, and thinking styles. They understand what other people think is important. They learn to negotiate, to consider new alternatives, to reach a consensus.

In classrooms valuing empathy and collaboration, children scurry to create joint greetings to send to their friends who are ill. Their

hands shoot up at the announcement, "We need a small group to . . . ." They volunteer to escort a new non–English-speaking child around school for a week. They look forward to choosing teams or serving on committees on

- **complicated projects,** such as planning a field trip (The children vote on where to go. Small groups make arrangements: select dates; set up transportation; talk with the person in charge about what is most interesting; map how to get there, noting landmarks to watch for; copy, distribute, and collect permission slips; enlist volunteer escorts; list questions for children to think about and main points to look for; keep track of each other during the trip; follow up by writing experience stories and thank-you notes, or drawing what they saw); and

- **everyday tasks,** such as unpacking a box of various types of drums or hauling in a laundry basket of assorted sand-digging implements supplied by children's families.

Sometimes groups form and then dissolve in a minute or two; other groups may work together for a week or more until their task is complete. Usually dynamic duos or thrilling trios are about as large as kindergartners can manage; by second grade, committees can be a bit larger.

Whenever possible, children choose the groups that appeal to them, but at times teachers may want to select committees with a greater purpose in mind. Perhaps one child could benefit under the wing of a strong leader. Maybe another needs a

> **Children work together best when they are mastering the basic skills— positive self-esteem, self-discipline, and democratic conflict resolution.**

gentle nudge to branch out with new friends or ideas.

Of course, children work together best when they are mastering the basic skills—positive self-esteem, self-discipline, and democratic conflict resolution. While children tackle their self-defined tasks, teachers float among groups, answer questions, obtain materials, ask thought-provoking questions, and stay tuned to the need for collaboration or division of overlapping tasks.

Academic skills thrive in a diverse classroom. Lest readers conclude that cooperative learning is all "play" and no "work," let us set the record straight: Cooperation results in mastery of content as well as social skills. Children learn math, languages, spelling, handwriting, science, and social studies when they work together to carry out hands-on, intriguing projects. They see how useful it is to know how to add when they are spending their own hard-earned money for stamps so they can send letters to a pen-pal class in a neighboring state. Imagine the incentive to spell correctly and to print neatly for such an important project!

Vocabularies expand as children explain their ideas, seek information from people and books, draw or write reports, or give brief talks on their findings. Logical thinking blossoms when children organize their own activities into a workable sequence, set their own priorities and timetables, and build convincing arguments for alternative solutions.

When small groups of children are asked to come up with several possible solutions, rather than to find one specific answer, they engage in real-world problem solving. Open-ended questions such as "Why do you think . . . ?" or "How would you go about . . . ?" encourage thinking. Peer tutoring—when one child assists another to understand a concept—also can benefit both children because, as

Children learn the most when they work together to solve real, meaningful problems.

we well know, teachers generally learn more from a project than students.

On the other hand, drilling a partner or correcting each other's worksheets does not reflect the spirit of genuinely cooperative learning, neither does merely following instructions to carry out a science experiment. Why? Thinking—is missing. Children learn the most when they work together to figure out real, meaningful problems. They learn best when learning suits their own purposes and needs, not those of some stranger. For more suggestions of topics that lend themselves well to cooperative learning, see especially Group projects, page 85, Chapter 6.

Family involvement

Programs that value children value their families. As we have already seen, by understanding children's family cultures, teachers can align children's experiences at home and school. Together, teachers and families support children's self-esteem and success—in school and beyond. This discussion briefly considers how families and teachers can share information and jointly work toward mutual educational goals for children in culturally and individually appropriate ways (Bredekamp, 1987).

Information sharing. Schools achieve continuity with children's homes when families and teachers exchange information about their mutual concern—the education of children. Information that is valuable for all parties includes children's interests, developmental patterns, language(s), family preferences, allergies, memorable experiences, styles of

Families should be gently encouraged to become partners in their children's education.

discipline, and expectations. All indicate important areas in which partnerships can be established on behalf of children.

Teachers *can* reach out to families in ways that respect their preferences and without prying into the families' affairs. All information obtained is held in professional confidence. As indicated earlier, addressing parents by name in the style of their culture is an essential first step (Morrow, 1989). Many families respond well to casual telephone conversations or notes. Some are pleased to have the teacher come to their homes. Others prefer to make impromptu classroom visits. Formal or informal conferences are the choice of still others. A number of families are honored to be invited to serve as regular or special occasion volunteers. Questionnaires (in the family's language) may appeal to others. Persistence and cordiality may be as important as the method used.

Some families may be more eager than others to become partners in their children's education, but teachers should gently encourage all. In some ethnic and low-income groups, parents have bitter memories about their school years and are skeptical about what may befall their own children (Herrera & Wooden, 1988). Still others, such as Head Start parents, are already empowered to actively seek community services. In Tulsa, an Effective Black Parenting program challenges parents to view their practices in a historical perspective and to learn practical ways to deal with their children in the 90s (Archer, 1990).

Teachers are also alert to families with diverse needs, including those who adopt or have interracial children (Wardle, 1987, 1990, 1992b; Hearst, 1993), or who are poten-

tially abusive (Meddin & Rosen, 1986), divided or blended (Skeen, Robinson, & Flake-Hobson, 1984), gay or lesbian (Clay, 1990; Corbett, 1993; Wickens, 1993), or substance abusive (Oyemade & Washington, 1989). These families, like all others, may be struggling with stress and would welcome respectful referrals to support groups or agencies.

Whatever the makeup of the family or method of information sharing, Greenberg recommends that "Each individual teacher . . . make a maximum feasible effort to reach the families of every child in the class—with respect" (1989, p. 68). Teachers who can communicate in, or are eager to learn, the families' languages demonstrate their commitment to offering a high-quality, relevant education for each child.

Reaching mutual education goals. Most parents and teachers find that they agree on goals for children similar to those identified at the outset of this book. These goals comprehensively address children's development while enabling teachers to take into account cultural and individual variations. Specific goals are also identified for each child by teachers and the child's family, as a team.

Conferences and other scheduled meetings offer concentrated times for children's most important people to get to know each other, to jointly set goals for children, and to discuss children's progress. These events are scheduled best at hours and places convenient to and comfortable for parents. If families and teachers do not speak a common language, an interpreter might assist. Establish a positive, caring tone, and if necessary, remember to use democratic conflict resolution to resolve disagreements.

When education starts with what young children know best—their families—they feel secure and ready to build on their knowledge. Children are usually eager to talk about their loved ones. They willingly draw and/or write about their families. Some like to bring family photos to school. Others will volunteer their nana to bring her great-grandmother's shawl or hat for the children to gingerly touch as part of a unit on family history. Curriculum ideas for individual and group projects about families are included in Chapter 6.

Family volunteers can be creatively included in children's activities, not just assigned mundane tasks or expected to show up for parent-teacher meetings. Recruit parents to carry out roles that make a genuine contribution to the diversity of their children's classrooms, such as these:

- share skills such as weaving or tortilla making;

- read stories or poems in their primary language;

- teach or perform songs, dances, or other facets of their culture;

- display family heirlooms, describing why their ancestors treasured the items;

- write children's dictated stories about their family histories;

- donate a cultural artifact to the school for a child's birthday or in honor of a teacher; and

- seek community resources (see Community contributions, this page).

How is children's educational progress evaluated by families and teachers who are partners? Grades and test scores inadequately communicate the real advances children demonstrate each day if we but observe closely: the once-shy child who now plays with others in the neighborhood and on the playground, the previously sullen child who cheerfully recycles paper at home and school, the former wiggler who writes expressive poetry.

Samples of children's writings, drawings, and projects, saved during the year,

graphically portray growth in muscle control, interests, vocabulary, and many other developments. Progress is measured for each child in many ways that only a family-teacher partnership can fully appreciate.

The importance of building respectful relationships with families and sharing educational goals is punctuated by experiences such as one from years ago described by a veteran teacher of young children:

> At the height of the civil rights demonstrations, a parent said to me, "You and me ain't never going to agree about niggers, Mrs. West. But I do know that you love my boy, so you won't teach him nothing that will hurt him." Having already established positive relations with the child and his parents, I could then explain that their son was growing up in a world that would be different from the world they had known, that the school was trying to prepare him to function in that world.
>
> In the most extreme cases, it may become necessary to say that parents have the right to teach their values to their children, but the school has the obligation to prepare children to function in a broader society. (West, 1992, pp. 138–139)

Community contributions

Successful schools build partnerships not only with families but within communities. Children go beyond the school to get acquainted with and demonstrate their concern for people. At the same time, community residents come into the school to share their experiences and talents with future generations. The primary years are perfect for engaging children's sense of respect for each other through community responsibility.

Children reach out. Every neighborhood contains possibilities for learning, whether the school building is located in the midst of the city or on a quiet country road. Children constantly learn from their surroundings if teachers take advantage of the resources: transportation, plants, shelter, weather, businesses, insects

Progress is measured for each child in ways that only a home-school partnership can fully appreciate.

and animals, food, pollution, and especially people.

Immerse children in their communities. Take walking trips, visit markets, tour industries, explore farms, ramble through flea markets, gaze at museum exhibits, listen to musicians practice, see artists in action, watch construction crews work, and marvel at radio or TV stations.

Excursions, of course, have little relevance unless children are prepared in advance and given ample opportunities to follow through with what they are learning. Let's examine how this process for fully involving children in the community works by seeing how they might study clothing

* * *

A clothing unit might be introduced by asking children to examine the similarities and differences in what they are wearing on a typical day. One group of children could record and then graph how many are wearing sneakers, leather shoes, sandals, boots, or other types of footwear; another group might graph outdoor wear if it's cold or rainy; one group might consider types of closures (buttons, snaps, elastic, zippers, laces, Velcro). Hats are always a hit, perhaps aided with the tale *Caps for Sale* (Slobodkina, 1948) or *Whose Hat Is That?* (Roy, 1990). Take photos to record what children are wearing or ask children to trace each other's outlines on large sheets of paper and have them "dress" themselves. Make footprints with shoe bottoms, using paint on newspaper or water on the sidewalk.

Children's horizons expand through hands-on activities. Provide paper dolls, doll clothing, and dress-up apparel from many ethnic groups. Arrange for children to try on, or at least gently feel, many types of fabrics sewn in many different styles. Perhaps families would be willing to model everyday apparel worn in their ancestor's homes, let children try on a pair of wooden shoes, or demonstrate how their sari is put on. Check with fabric stores, second-hand stores, theater groups, costume designers, quilters, and others in the area to obtain

Children are *participants* in making the community a better place to live.

samples of contemporary and historical cloth and clothing.

Children could calculate how much their outfit or wardrobe costs by using a catalog. Or they could set up a pretend telephone ordering department, and call in orders to each other. Collect magazines and children's books from different countries and eras so children can compare colors, fabrics, and styles. Family pictures are another good source for observing the types of clothing people wear. How do you dress for special occasions? What do you wear to the beach? The Americans All photos, and the Augustus Sherman collection in particular, contain a wide variety of historical prints that offer a fascinating glimpse into clothing design.

Help children recognize how climate, natural resources, fads, cultural influences, and personal preferences affect what people wear. Children could survey passers-by, noting what they are wearing and conjecturing why (a hard hat might be worn by a construction worker, children with boots might be ready to play in the snow).

Use children's literature—that contains elements dealing with clothing—as a jumping off point. Perhaps children will become so involved they'll produce a play; or maybe they'll find or paint pictures of the kinds of clothing people in many different cultures wear when they dance. See the listing of children's books in Part 3 for a few inspiring titles.

By this time, children have enough background information to benefit from an excursion—maybe to a wardrobe museum, a used clothing store (where children will probably be free to touch), or a department store. Ask children to decide what they will look for, feel, or listen for during their tour. What kinds of jobs do people do there? What do they need to know to do their jobs? Who shops in this store? Who wore the costumes? Children can generate questions to ask their guides.

When children return to their classroom, they are eager to talk about what impressed them. They'll probably raise more questions, initiating yet another library search or requiring a telephone call. Children might write and illustrate their own books about what happened on field trips. And of course, either individually or as a group, thank-you notes are carefully composed by the children, edited by each other, and then copied in the children's best penmanship. Thanks go to bus driver, chaperones, and tour guides.

As a continuing follow-up of the visit, children might get interested in sewing. Who could teach them? Which businesses might donate materials? Yarn, burlap, or nylon net and large-eye needles make it possible for beginners to successfully experiment and create. Or children might want to find out where fabric comes from, and a study of sheep or cotton is in order. How is fabric made? Bring out the handmade looms, a spin-

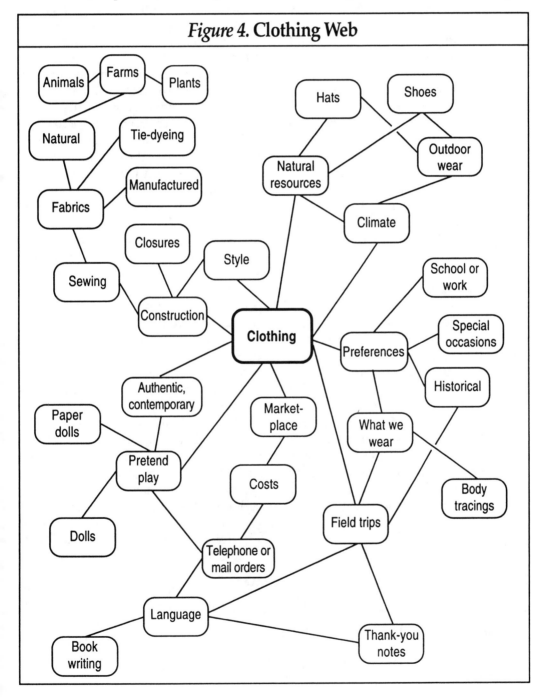

Figure 4. Clothing Web

ning wheel. The web of learning never ends, once children are tuned in to all there is to know about everyday topics that interest them.

* * *

Whatever the topic, when children and teachers put their heads together, the community becomes a rich resource for children to learn about the marvels of the people who live and work nearby. What unusual—or everyday—places capture children's curious, adventuresome spirits?

Community involvement means children are more than just spectators. They are *participants* in making the community a better place to live. They regularly read stories and sing songs with a group of residents at an elder-care facility. They join the crew for a park cleanup. They design posters to recruit blood donors. They repair donated toys for redistribution. They display their artwork during the Week of the Young Child. For the spring elementary band concert, children illustrate programs, usher, and move chairs.

Communities are part of the schools. Schools are the essence of a community, because schools nurture the next generation of parents, workers, and leaders that will ensure the area's future. Schools today bravely make overtures to their community, if it hasn't already rallied around the schools.

Where to start? Ask a small business or a civic group to adopt a classroom. Arrange with a larger group, such as a major employer or chain store, to adopt a building. When the community's investment is personalized (rather than just writing a property-tax check), and when children and volunteers get acquainted, commitment to the value of education deepens for everyone involved. Adults, just like children, learn best through hands-on experiences!

Corporate and individual volunteers are adding their much-needed energy to ensure that children receive every benefit possible from their fleeting years in the community's schools. Business-education partnerships offer tutoring services, grants-fund special projects, or staff to give children attention they deserve. Literacy programs, such as Reading Is Fundamental, thrive. Substance abuse prevention programs are sponsored by coalitions of local organizations who recognize the importance of children's dreams for success.

Time, talent, materials, and financial resources are critical elements that communities can supply to improve the quality of America's education. Check with administrators about what community services are offered to schools. Identify needs for individual classrooms or entire buildings—involve children, families, and staff. All can pool their perceptions to prepare lists of pressing needs, establish priorities, and adopt strategies to obtain critical resources for learning. Children can sometimes be their own best advocates when they are treated with respect and involved in meaningful ways.

Resources are everywhere. A lumber yard or cabinet shop donates wood scraps so children can learn carpentry skills. Families save beautiful junk, such as paper towel rolls and small boxes, for children's construction and art projects. Offices recycle paper and other supplies to schools. Empty-nesters read to children on their laps. Retirees screen children for potential vision or hearing problems. Hobbyists show children how to tie knots or take care of potted plants. Grocery stores act as drop-off points for recycling aluminum cans—the proceeds of which are donated to schools.

Involve communities in classrooms and watch curricula come alive for all!

When the community's investment is personalized, and when children and volunteers get acquainted, commitment to the value of education deepens.

Chapter 6

Curriculum Ideas

Teaching strategies to facilitate children's thinking in diverse directions are scattered throughout this guide. Most of the ideas introduced in this chapter hinge on background materials presented earlier, so readers who tend to look at the back of the book for the most practical ideas are encouraged to begin at the front of this one!

Harmonious integration of content and relevance to children's lives—as opposed to fragmentation into traditional subjects and meaninglessness—are the hallmarks of any individually and culturally appropriate curriculum:

> The curriculum embraces the reality of multiculturalism in American society by providing a balance between learning the common core of dominant cultural knowledge (for example, the English language, democratic values) and knowledge of minority cultures. Curriculum accommodates children who have limited English proficiency. All the cultures and primary languages of the children are respectfully reflected in the curriculum. (NAEYC & NAECS/SDE, 1991, p. 30)

Although there are many curriculum design approaches to take, themes often enable teachers to carry out specific activities that provide balance and adaptability. Some themes that appeal to—and make sense to—young children and lend themselves well to a broadened understanding of human nature are offered in Table 10. As we have seen, themes are best developed by planning—*with* children, rather than *for* them—through a web of ideas that can be explored in small groups and by individuals (Katz & Chard, 1989).

Appropriate topics and opportunities

> It is certainly true that history cannot satisfy our appetite when we are hungry, nor keep us warm when the cold wind blows. But it is also true that if younger generations do not understand the hardships and triumphs of their elders, then we will be a people without a past. As such, we will be like water without a source, a tree without roots.
>
> —*New York Chinatown History Project*

Every good teacher gradually accumulates a unique set of materials that children, parents, and colleagues alike can use to develop a fuller grasp of our patchwork-quilt diversity and history as a country. Each colorful patch in that quilt, each tiny stitch, the fluffy stuffing, and the strong backing all are essential to form the American quilt that holds us together as one nation.

Table 10. Samples of Themes That Incorporate Diversity Into the Curriculum

Families

People live in many kinds of families

Every family has a history

People use written and spoken language to communicate

Families teach their children what they value

Every family has traditions

Families help each other

Work

People work together at home

People work with each other in many places

People do many kinds of jobs

Some people work for fairness so others might have better lives

Housing

People live in a variety of homes

Types of homes are affected by weather, building materials available, local history, and many other factors

Individual and Group Similarities and Differences

People all need food, clothing, shelter, and each other

Physical features vary among individuals and between ethnic and racial groups

People dress, eat, work, and live in ways that vary by culture

Clothing (see Figure 4)

Food

Foods help us grow and stay healthy

Cultures and families have different food preferences and eating habits

Foods grow in different climates

Foods are prepared in many ways

Food is a precious natural resource

Fine Arts

Cultural and individual expressions are found in music, poetry, literature, and many types of art

People create their own art

People enjoy each other's art

Children are drawn to different topics and various teaching methods. Therefore, a variety of types of resources provides teachers with flexibility and the potential to individualize the curriculum so that each child gains the most from her or his early years. This chapter offers a few ideas for incorporating some topics and items that are the most appropriate for young children into everyday classroom activities. Use these suggestions, many of which build on the Americans All program, as well as items collected through the years, to launch activities that are a perfect match for each group of children!

Teacher resource materials. Read journals and books that deal with experiences of ethnic groups represented in your own communities. A broad perspective of the hurdles and triumphs people faced in the shaping of America enables teachers to better understand children (Zinn, 1980; Miner, 1992–93). There is so much more to our national heritage than most of us ever memorized in history class! Better yet, explore how the history of our nation overlaps events worldwide! When history comes alive for you, it will come alive for the children in the group.

Children's books. An increasing number of delightful books designed for children recount people's own cultural, personal, and family stories with authentic pictures. Some books focus on diversity, others include it as part of a broader story line. Here are some titles that might be interesting to start with:

How My Parents Learned To Eat (Friedman, 1984)
Family Pictures (Garza, 1990)
Africa Dream (Greenfield, 1989)
Hector Lives in the U.S. Now: The Story of a Mexican-American Child (Hewett, 1990)
Aunt Flossie's Hats (& Crab Cakes Later) (Howard, 1991)

Harmonious integration of content and relevance to children's lives are the hallmarks of any individually and culturally appropriate curriculum.

My First American Friend (Jin, 1991)
An Arctic Community (Kalman & Belsey, 1988)
How My Family Lives in America (Kuklin, 1992)
The People Shall Continue (Ortiz, 1988)
Tree of Cranes (Say, 1991)
People of the Breaking Day (Sewall, 1990)
All Kinds of Families (Simon, 1975)
Got Me A Story To Tell: Five Children Tell About Their Lives (Yee & Kokin, 1977)

Work with families to help children prepare similar materials about their individual stories as well.

When introducing books that include diversity, teachers, volunteers, or older children might read just one story or section at a time to the youngest children. One idea is usually sufficient to begin or expand the study of a specific cultural group or historical event. By second grade, some children might be interested in listening to an adult read through an entire collection; others may read independently.

Children's books supplement social studies units on topics such as transportation or homes, for example. They explain the settings of other works of children's fiction such as Cohlene (1990) or Mathieu (1979) or historical materials in any up-to-date reading series. Books that include diversity are naturals to be incorporated as part of science study about crops, animals, or foods (Morris, 1989).

Historical dates mean little to young children without ties to events in their own lives, so teachers should explain material in ways that match children's experiences. Comments such as "Long, long ago, before your grandparents were

born . . . " or "In the olden days, when airplanes and telephones hadn't been invented yet . . . " will lend a bit of context for children who have always known TV, computers, and fax machines, and who may have difficulty imagining a world in which travel was on foot and communication was without telephone. Historical photos and drawings are excellent helps for building these bridges, as is the information about historical peoples (Tables 11 through 16).

However children's books are incorporated into the curriculum, there are always many new concepts and vocabulary words to grasp—and ideas to expand upon—so tie them closely to the hands-on items found in each classroom. Tools, jewelry, coins, hats, and many cultural artifacts—as well as field trips and visitors—can be interwoven through fiction and nonfiction, and will bring children's awareness of diversity into the present and future. Ask children to add to the stories on their own, to illustrate their ideas, or to find other pictures to help explain topics.

Children's responses to open-ended questions will help teachers discern just how well main ideas—such as reservations, slavery, prison camps, colonies, freedom, and cultural customs—are understood by the children. Questions such as "What do you think happened to Japanese Americans while they were in prison camp?" might reveal that children think the prisoners had a good time toasting marshmallows, because that's what camp means to some children! Use clues such as these to seek out additional information and activities to broaden children's knowledge base.

Supplement books with an abundance of historical and contemporary resources about children and families in each cul-

Tie stories closely to the hands-on items in each classroom.

tural group, such as videos (perhaps portions of the PBS Civil War series), maps, dramatic play props, art projects, storytellers, cooking experiences, music, and community activities. Relate the material to children's lives, and they begin to grasp how history is made.

By picking up on children's curiosity about events—perhaps the treacherous ship voyages that many peoples endured or the many uses for the buffalo—entire webs of activities can be constructed to bring brief stories to life for children, and thus help them tie their histories together as Americans all.

Photographs. Americans All has compiled an elegant set of photographs depicting the life and times of earlier America. The Augustus Sherman immigrant portraits within the Americans All Photograph Collection intrigue adults and children alike. If you do not have access to this collection through your curriculum specialist or school system, begin to build your own resource file of historic and contemporary photos of children. Two of the best resources for photos are catalogs of children's clothing and toys, and magazines. Color posters from the National Association for the Education of Young Children and calendars with photos of diverse people are excellent to hang around the room. With a watchful eye, you'll soon have a large selection of your own prints; when you pool yours with colleagues, the collection will be even larger.

Draw children's attention to details in the photos, such as the objects they can identify in the tenement in Photo 359 of the Americans All collection. Ask thought-provoking questions such as "What do you think is hap-

Draw children's attention to details in photos.

Table 11. Native Americans*

Native American words we use today

Animals: raccoon, coyote, bison (buffalo)

Foods: squash, tomato, potato, tapioca, chocolate, succotash, barbecue

Things: hammock, canoe, moccasin, totem, hurricane

Places: Seattle (Photo 239), Iowa, Sioux, Cherokee, Cheyenne, Omaha, Delaware
These are just a few words from the 200 Native American languages that are still spoken in parts of the United States and Canada.

Photos of special interest to young children

Zuni pueblo (Photo 223): Note oven, roof terraces, wall finishings. Discuss building materials, land forms, uses of ladders, food prepared in oven.

Bison roaming (Photo 230): Buffalo were used for food, clothing, lodging, and tools. When the buffalo were killed off by immigrants, Native Americans were robbed of their primary means of survival. Discover more about buffalo. What parts were used for food? How was clothing made? What was used for lodging? What kinds of tools were carved? How big were buffalo? How were they killed? What animals do people rely on today?

Children at the Zuni Pueblo school (Photo 232)

Omaha boys at the Carlisle, Pennsylvania, Indian School (Photo 233): The man in charge of the school said its purpose was "to civilize the Indian, get him into civilization." How do you think Native Americans, who had their own schools, language, culture, values, and reverence for the earth, felt about being called uncivilized? Ask children to compare how children's faces, hair, and clothing differ between Photos 232 and 233. Discuss how children felt to be taken from their families and robbed of their culture.

Angeline, a Duwamish (Photo 239): Her father was Chief Seattle, after whom the city in Washington was named. Can children identify any local Native American names for states, cities, counties, rivers, and lakes? Which nations lived in the area? How did they live in harmony with the land? What happened to them?

Activity: Some famous Native Americans

Biographies of some of these famous Native Americans, or stories about those who were everyday heroes or heroines, past and present, can be read with children regularly.

Sacajawea (Shoshoni): Assisted Lewis and Clark on their river expedition.

Chief Sara Winnemucca (Paiute): Urged the U.S. government to improve its treatment of Native Americans. (Photo 238)

Dr. Susan LaFlesche Picotte (Omaha): Physician and first woman leader of her nation. (Photo 237)

Chief Joseph (Nez Perce, Photo 225), *Chief Plenty Coups* (Crow, Photo 226), *Big Foot* (Miniconjou Dakota), *Geronimo* (Chiricahua Apache, with General Cook in Photo 229): Defended their people's land.

Table 12. African Americans[*]

Africa lives on in American culture

West African or Bantu words: tote, OK, bozo, zombie

Foods: jambalaya, gumbo, dumplings, coffee, yams

Music: banjo, drums, jazz, calypso

Fashions: cornrows

Folk tales: Uncle Remus Tales

Photos of special interest to young children

School children (Photo 394): When America's Civil War ended, young African American children were sent to school for the first time. Many of these schools were run by missionaries and other abolitionists. Although children did learn to read and write, much of their time was spent learning practical skills. What are these children learning? Why? What kinds of practical things do children learn in school today?

Gathering and spinning cotton (Photo 406): Children can compare this process to the way wool is handled (Photo 326 and Lasky, 1980). Obtain cotton bolls, discuss climate needed to grow cotton, sew with cotton, compare feel of cotton with other fabrics. Talk about what hard work it was to grow and pick cotton by hand (children may not be aware that cotton pickers with engines were not used then).

Activity: Meet two enslaved African Americans who gained their freedom

Frederick Douglass: The son of an enslaved African American and a European American father, Douglass (Photo 392) chose his name from a book. He escaped from slavery in Baltimore in 1838. He was a powerful speaker against slavery. After he published his autobiography, he had to flee to England to escape recapture. His English friends purchased his freedom. Douglass returned to New York and founded a newspaper. He was active in the Underground Railroad. His home in Washington, D.C., is open to visitors.

Sojourner Truth: Truth (Photo 391) was given the name Isabella when she was born to an African American slave in New York in 1797. Isabella had several masters before she was freed from slavery by state law. In 1843 she adopted the name Sojourner Truth and began to travel across the North. She earned money by giving speeches and selling her autobiography. She talked about how important it was to free enslaved African Americans and to allow women to vote. During the Civil War she helped care for wounded soldiers and newly freed African Americans. She urged her people to own land and learn to read.

---

[*]Photo numbers in Tables 11–16 refer to selections in the Americans All Photograph Collection, a set of 262 photographs with descriptions, available in the *Individual Teacher's Resource Package* for grades K–2 or 3–4 from Americans All, a national education program. The photo set is available separately from The Portfolio Project, Inc., 6011 Blair Rd., N.W., Washington, DC 20011 (phone 202–832–0330).

Table 13. Asian Americans*

Teachers are urged to help children think of each Asian group separately, because each has its own history, culture, language, and unique experiences in America. In addition, focus on contemporary contributions made by past and recent immigrants from Asian countries.

Photos of special interest to young children

Railroad workers (Photo 263): Many Chinese immigrants first found work by helping to build railroads. What materials were used? How did the land have to be changed? Take a train ride. Build railroad trestles with blocks and sand.

Saiji Kimura's store (Photo 276): Japanese immigrants came to Hawaii expecting to work a short time in the sugar industry, but as more workers stayed in Hawaii, some immigrants began to open businesses of their own. What kinds of products do you imagine were stocked in this store? How would the goods get from Japan to the United States?

Inez Cayaban, a nurse (Photo 288): Filipino music still has its own Pinoy touch. Cabayan and her husband entertained soldiers during World War II. Listen to some authentic Filipino music. What instruments are used?

Marina Estrella Espina (Photo 293): Espina is a librarian at the University of New Orleans who immigrated to the United States with her family in 1967. She studies early Filipino history in America, and gives speeches on U.S.-Philippine relations as well as librarianship.

Table 14. European Americans*

Much of U.S. history has concentrated on European perspectives, so resources for these groups—from museums to architecture—abound in most communities. Americans All offers a balanced approach, giving children an opportunity to grasp the enduring contributions of many ethnic and cultural groups to the building of America.

Photos of special interest to young children

Tenement (Photo 359): Many European American families were large and lived in small quarters. Immigrants early in this century lived in conditions similar to this. How is this scene similar to homes you know? How is it different?

Children at work (Photo 360): Young immigrant children worked in cities and on farms. Five-year-old Salvin is carrying two pecks of cranberries to the delivery station in New Jersey. Newsboys in Philadelphia are selling papers; other children are selling candy and gum on the streets. Why do you think child labor is no longer allowed?

Table 15. Mexican Americans*

Spanish words that are part of our culture

silo, fiesta, patio, cafeteria, bonanza, chili

Photos of special interest to young children

Sheep-shearing crew with wool bagged for Galveston, Texas (Photo 326): Watch a sheep being sheared. How long does it take to shear a sheep? How many sheep's wool would fit in one of these bags? What happens to the wool?

Family moving (Photo 328): When Mexican Americans were forced off their lands, they had to load their belongings into a wagon and look for a new homestead. Children were often given the responsibility of herding livestock behind the wagon. Notice the type of architecture, the street. How is moving a family different today?

Activity: Portrait of a Mexican American journalist

Jovita Idar (Photo 330): A crusader, Idar spoke out about the problems of Mexican Americans in her articles in an important Spanish-language newspaper in Texas. In this photo of the print shop, she is the second person on the right.

Idar was more than a writer. She was an activist, too. In 1911 she and her family organized a major educational and cultural conference. One month later, she co-founded La Liga Femenil Mexicanista (the League of Mexican Women). This group worked to improve education for children from low-income families. During the Mexican Revolution, she organized La Cruz Blanca (the White Cross) to care for those wounded in battle.

Men and women such as Jovita Idar continue to stand up for the culture and rights of Mexican Americans.

Table 16. Puerto Ricans*

Photos of special interest to young children

Pablo Velez Rivera (Photo 441): Rivera came to work in a copper mine in Utah during World War II. He is about to drink a cup of Puerto Rican coffee made from beans sent to him by his friends back home. How do you think his family feels to be in Utah? What kinds of drinks do you like? How are they made?

Learning to vote with a machine in 1959 (Photo 451): Use this same democratic process as children make classroom decisions. Visit polling places; study candidates and issues.

---

*Photo numbers in Tables 11–16 refer to selections in the Americans All Photograph Collection, a set of 262 photographs with descriptions, available in the *Individual Teacher's Resource Package* for grades K–2 or 3–4 from Americans All, a national education program. The photo set is available separately from The Portfolio Project, Inc., 6011 Blair Rd., N.W., Washington, DC 20011 (phone 202–832–0330).

pening here? Why is the child looking away from the table? Why do you think these people lived together in one place?"

Use the photos you collect to help illustrate other reading materials children encounter. In addition, children might select one or more photos that especially appeal to them. They could write (or dictate to a volunteer or on tape) a story telling their ideas about the people in the photo: how they got there, what they were doing, and what eventually happened to them. This could be done before or after giving children the background information about the photo. Encourage children to illustrate their story to show how life has changed since the photo was taken.

Children also enjoy taking their own photographs, either of family or friends, to document their personal histories. The more cameras and film the merrier! With a bit of assistance, children can see how photographers get fairly close to capture people's facial expressions, their clothing, their hands, or some other interesting feature. A volunteer might take a small group of children out to the school playground, a park, or a store to record the variety of people in the community.

Families might share some carefully displayed photographs of ancestors. And of course, teachers will want to record children involved in the great adventure of learning about each other. Use group and individual scrapbooks, create frames, put together an exhibit, submit photos to the local paper, create a classroom newsletter complete with photos—the possibilities for building upon photography of people are endless.

Timelines. A compact timeline, such as the one assembled for Americans All, weaves the threads of human history as never before. At a glance, adults can see how events around the world shaped the changing human landscape. Teachers are

Primary children can begin to understand the use of timelines to depict passage of time and the crucial events that occur in people's histories.

urged to become thoroughly familiar with this timeline, or similar information, as a baseline for selecting accurate materials and topics.

Although primary children generally will find detailed timelines far beyond their grasp, older-age classes can begin to understand the use of these tools to depict the passage of time and the crucial events that occur in people's histories. Highlights of events in U.S. history are translated for children by relating the happenings to children's own lives whenever appropriate situations arise. What groups of people are likely to have picked the oranges they had for lunch? Why did these peoples come to America? How long have they been here?

Perhaps most importantly, even the youngest children can begin to construct timelines for their own lives. Such a project will most likely involve their families, who can contribute major events to list. A month-by-month timeline might work best for primary-age children, because parents often remember details such as "You first walked when you were 11 months old. You said 'Mama' at 18 months. You were 5 years and 2 months when you started kindergarten." Use long stretches of paper so that children have plenty of space to write captions or illustrate the hallmarks in their own lives. Recycled continuous-feed computer paper works perfectly for the task.

Older primary children might want to begin a timeline for their class, marking important dates such as when their families arrived in America, when they were born, and when their school was built. Their timeline might be marked out with blocks in the classroom or on a long strip of paper down the hallway, or on the playground. Think of the measurement and planning involved to assure that dates are properly spaced! Consider the language experiences as children phrase their entries and write them for all to read!

Maps. World maps are just beginning to make sense to second graders, so maps are primarily for adults to further their understanding of movement patterns of various cultural groups. Many children may be curious about Native American nations whose peoples lived in their own area, and where they live now and why they moved. The September 1992 issue of *Young Children* includes detailed information about America's indigenous peoples.

Most children in the group will probably have moved from one home to another, so explore the ideas of moving and mapping. Use children's experiences and concerns to construct a web of learning

There's so much to extract from children's lives that integrates with diversity!

activities about moving. Why do people move? What plans are needed? How are boxes packed? What does it cost to rent a truck? How long does it take to drive? Watch movers hauling furniture from home to truck. What happens to old friends? How did people move in earlier times? Find photos of contemporary moves. Americans All Photos 57, 224, 328, 362, and 410 correlate with this topic.

As was discussed in Part 1, early mapping skills are fostered when children use blocks to represent their classrooms, their homes, their neighborhoods, or entire cities. Draw area maps with markers on a large plain bed sheet. Children can add

buildings made from cardboard boxes or blocks; toy vehicles can travel the streets. To help children see how valuable hand-drawn maps can be, use them to locate field trip destinations.

Perhaps some older children will want to use world, national, or state maps to trace their own families' movement patterns. Obtain a city or county map to plot local moves. Again, blocks or boxes can become the stuff of which children's homes are made. There's so much to extract from children's everyday lives that can be directly integrated with diversity discussions and materials!

Music. Teachers and school staff members and families find music a natural way to get involved in diversity because music spans all cultures and times (New World Records, 1976; Delacre, 1989; Mattox, 1989; Sweet Honey in the Rock, 1990). Families are usually willing to share recordings, instruments, or books that reflect their musical heritages. Children easily learn other languages when they sing traditional songs their friends know. Music is one resource that can be called upon every day whenever the mood strikes!

Music and gym teachers can incorporate authentic cultural songs and dances in their curricula. Ask art teachers for assistance in encouraging children to create their own instruments, such as maracas from the Caribbean (Schuman, 1981). Collaborate with teachers of older children, whose groups might be willing to record songs for younger children to learn by listening. Older children or family members may also be available to accompany the primary grades, using autoharps, drums, or guitars. A simple friendship dance, in which children move in a circle to the beat of a drum, establishes a unifying atmosphere.

Music can spread children's wings to include the entire community. Invite performers not only to play or dance but to

Music can spread children's wings to include the entire community.

talk with children about their music and to involve children in the making of it. Children can try their hand at new instruments, don apparel worn for dancing, and begin to appreciate the wide range of musical expressions that characterize America and the world.

Posters. Proudly hang posters and children's artwork related to diversity in classrooms, hallways, resource rooms, administrative offices, and proclaim to children, families, and the public that children are growing in their commitment to human history and values. Displays are perfect for calling attention to the results of discussions about children's stories, drawings, and photos.

Books. In-depth materials about ethnic and cultural groups are available from a variety of resources, including Americans All. Although highlights of information—myths and realities—from these resources are featured in Part 1 of this guide, teachers are urged to read further to gain a broader appreciation for the triumphs and setbacks each group has faced in this country.

Additional background information of great interest to young children, some suggested questions for children to consider, and a few extra ideas are provided in Tables 11 through 16 so that teachers can begin to bridge this information with children's experiences. Photo numbers match the Americans All materials, but other sources exist for similar pictures.

Help children recognize common threads—such as the enslavement of people of several ethnic groups, or low-paying first jobs that provided basic services such as food, clothing, or transportation—in their histories. Creative teachers easily find many ways to build upon these suggestions and to ferret out more information.

Learning activities for young children

Real-life stories and adventure make diversity and history personal and interesting for adults and children alike. Children's interests, cultures, and individual learning styles ensure that every class is unlike any other classroom. We also know that primary children are eager to take on responsibilities that match their developmental capabilities. Armed with this awareness, teachers can develop curricula that fit children, rather than trying to force children to follow a set of activities prescribed by strangers.

Help children recognize common threads in their histories.

Throughout this guide, we offer suggestions for a wide range of learning activities, but only teachers know which ones will appeal to their specific children. We present, then, a final sampling of individual and group ideas that might spark the gleam in a child's eye and lead to a lifetime of success and learning about—and appreciation for—self and others. For more specific learning activities that value diversity, see McCracken (1990, 1992).

Individual activities

Although these hands-on activities start with one or more children doing their own research to solve real problems, they might well blossom into group activities when friends find out what exciting events are underway!

Personal projects. Find out what interests each child—sewing, dance, drums, foods, gardening—and encourage children to pursue in-depth, individual experiences that naturally incorporate the overlapping skills of subjects such as reading, math, social studies, music, science, and health. Locate community experts who are willing to volunteer to teach children skills such as carving, weaving, or another language.

Leaders like me. Children find out more about heroines and heroes from their own culture, past and present, national and local. What qualities did these leaders exhibit? How did they help people? Who are the leaders now? How can children follow their examples?

Names. Build on children's abiding interest in their own names (Seefeldt, 1984; Morrow, 1989). In kindergarten, children learn to write their names, beginning with capital letters and then lowercase. Their names grace cubbies and rugs for circle time. Insert children's names into poetry or tunes such as "B-I-N-G-O" or "Johnny Hammers with One Hammer."

Some children are curious about the history and meaning of their names; perhaps their names changed when their families immigrated or migrated to a new community. Some may be named in memory of a beloved relative. Involve parents in children's quest for information about how they came to be named.

Family history. Urge families to share family history with their children, especially stories involving the children or their parents. Instead of reading a bedtime story, parents might recall events that happened before or after the child was born. Oral and written histories are great.

Perhaps a parent could help write a brief family history in the child's home language. By second grade, children can become their own reporters, taking notes and then writing their stories. They could illustrate the stories with their art work, perhaps done in styles consistent with their cultures. Some families might want to tape record or even videotape their sagas. Perhaps a mural, a photo album, or note cards would work better. Experiment with different formats for recording children's own life stories.

Family trees. Children could prepare their own family trees (Weitzman, 1975; Wolfman, 1991). Encourage them to interview family members and to enlist their assistance in putting the information in writing. Children might frame their family trees as gifts.

Proverbs and traditions. Ask children to talk with their families about cultural proverbs or family traditions. Choose one universal topic, such as love, birthdays, harvest festivals, responsibility, or time. Chart the responses, perhaps, to explore how different cultures express similar ideas. Children might also be fascinated to compare the different names they use for their grandparents (Williams, 1989). Listen and watch for children's comments that can lead to discoveries about each other.

Diaries. Older children could begin to write journals at home and at school about their own experiences (Abramson, Seda, & Johnson, 1990). Be sure to explain to

Celebrate!

- **milestones in children's own lives,**
- **growth in children's learning,**
- **children and their families, and**
- **world events.**

(Based on Neugebauer, 1990)

---

parents that invented spellings are perfectly fine—the object is for children to express their ideas. Children can dictate their entries to volunteers until they develop the skills to write their own journals.

Some older children might even like to write first-person accounts of other people's experiences. For example, they might imagine a diary written by a Chinese worker on the transcontinental railroad or children who lived in tenements or Native American, Chinese American, or Mexican American children whose parents were forced to work without any choices.

Group projects

Small, fluid groups are usually best for young children, with occasional efforts that capture the energy of the entire class. Group projects tend to focus on shared stories and histories and antibias contemporary issues (Derman-Sparks & the A.B.C. Task Force, 1989).

Small groups can tackle broad topics such as science (space, plant growing); social studies (parts of cities, countries, or farms); art (group collages); music (songs, dance); language (stories, plays, poetry, fingerplays); and health (growing foods) (Little Soldier, 1989). Pick up on what children are talking about with each other and expand their ideas.

Holidays—from New Year's to birthdays to Kwanzaa—have traditionally been used to study other cultures (Ramsey, 1979; McCracken, 1990; Wardle, 1990b). All too often, however, "by focusing on holidays we give children the impression that other people spend their time in ceremony, instead of going to work, raising children—living" (Derman-Sparks, 1992, p. 7).

In fact, stereotypes and myths are often unwittingly perpetuated when holidays are celebrated as the focus for study of culture. For example, most likely there was no Thanksgiving with Pilgrims and Native Americans (Ramsey, 1979; McCracken, 1990; Bigelow, Miner, & Peterson, 1991; Slapin & Seale, 1992). Children may be so hyped about Halloween that they fail to concentrate for days. Besides, families already celebrate those holidays that are important to them, so is it necessary for schools to duplicate efforts?

Teachers can eliminate these artificial perspectives of life past and present, and reduce the subtle or blatant messages conveyed by the holidays chosen for celebration. How? Neugebauer (1990) suggests that instead of celebrating ordinary holidays, far less fanfare and commercialization will result if children and their teachers quietly celebrate

- *milestones in children's own lives*—losing a tooth, growing out of a pair of shoes;
- *growth in children's learning*—reading a book independently, figuring out how to keep score, finishing a difficult puzzle;
- *children and their families*—a visit from a grandparent, the birth of a sibling, moving; and
- *world events*—volcanic eruptions, peace treaties, the first snowflake.

When this more personal approach is taken, children appreciate each day. They begin to grasp the scope of human interdependence in healthy, developmentally appropriate ways. These are some possibilities for carrying out this more professional style of teaching with groups of young children.

Getting to know you. We have seen how important it is to warmly welcome children and help them get acquainted with each other. Early in the school term, children might do self-portraits showing their favorite foods, songs, or stories. Children who work in pairs or trios are bound to get to know each other well.

Class book. Children like to record things they do together. They're collectors of photos, brochures, or memorabilia from field trip sites and their own stories (Neugebauer, 1992). Start them off on the first day you're together, and watch the volume of memories grow! What a great way to document children's progress through the year!

Dramatic events in history. Given sufficient contextual background, children can reenact historical events such as immigrants coming on a ship from Japan, China, the Philippines, Europe, or Africa; and the reactions to their arrival by Native Americans who had already lived here for generations. Take a covered-wagon ride across the country. Stage the Montgomery Bus boycott (Clemens, 1988; McCracken, 1990). Walk the Trail of Tears. Relive experiences of Filipino or Native American children who were uprooted from their families to attend schools far from home. These activities will capture children's hearts and imaginations!

Strive for simplicity and authenticity so that children can gain an understanding of the adventure, risks, and suffering that characterize so many Americans' experiences. Children can crowd into a small space to understand conditions on board

slave or passenger ships (see Americans All Photos 43, 166, 387, and 417). Play a recording of Martin Luther King, Jr.'s "I Have a Dream" speech. Ask individuals to volunteer to play key people such as Rosa Parks.

Committees of children can organize people and simple props; they can write brief scripts and schedules. What did ship passengers carry with them? How long did the voyage take? What did passengers do on board (remember, many were held captive for the journey)?

Reenactments are not intended to be performances to show off to others, or to cause children undue distress. Rather, they are conceived to give children a growing sense of how people live their own histories. As children traverse city streets or the playground, they step into the shoes, moccasins, or bare feet of others and gain a better understanding of the people who have gone before them. Heroes and heroines—recognized and unknown—continue to make our country great.

Snacks. Children get involved when they prepare snacks from various cultures. Popcorn was introduced to immigrants by Native Americans (Little Soldier, 1989). Read *Corn Is Maise* (Aliki, 1976). Find popcorn on the cob so children can shell their own. Experiment with ways to get the chaff out. Concoct a batch of gumbo (African American) or chili (Mexican American). Children can make a list of their snack choices, ask parents for recipes, find ways to earn money to purchase supplies, shop, and prepare the food. They might even grow their own pumpkins or potatoes if teachers collaborate from spring through fall!

International potluck. Children can help arrange a potluck dinner for the classroom—or an entire grade level or the school! Create a festive mood with displays of children's art. Each family brings a cherished ethnic dish to taste. After dinner, share some of the children's favorite songs, or encourage children to read beloved poems or stories about their heritage. To follow up, children can use computers to compile a recipe book. Encourage the use of children's home language in all the activities.

Time capsule. Little Soldier (1989) recommends that children assemble a collection of objects (or pictures cut from magazines for some items!) from contemporary American life into a time capsule. Ask children to think about why they chose those objects.

Newspapers, magazines, and catalogs. Children are often intrigued to compare household or clothing items from various cultures and time periods. Try to obtain a reproduction of a mail-order catalog from the turn of the century, or copies of old newspapers, so children can compare articles available and their prices with those of today. Even a 10-year-old catalog could be an eye opener!

Games. Children enjoy playing games that originated from many cultures (Kamii & DeVries, 1980; Hatcher, Pape, & Nicosia, 1988). Ask families for suggestions. Revise rules as needed to promote thinking and cooperation. Create all types of new games and encourage children to devise their own, too.

*   *   *

I hope these ideas spark the imaginations of children and teachers alike! Young children are far more likely to succeed in school and in life when we offer them a myriad of developmentally appropriate learning experiences throughout their early years.

As we all, as Americans, more fully comprehend our interwoven heritages, our diverse population can proudly come together—united as a nation and committed to realizing the ideals of democracy, truth, and fairness. Our collective strength lies in knowledge and understanding—about ourselves and each other.

> Prejudices, it is well known, are most difficult to eradicate from the heart whose soil has never been loosened or fertilized by education: they grow there, firm as weeds among stones.
>
> —*Charlotte Bronte*

Part **3**

Professional Resources

T hese selected listings are just a few of the vast number of printed resources available to children and educators who are eager to learn about themselves and each other. Why books? One of the all-time best African American writers for children expresses it this way:

> Not only do we as human beings have limitations—so also does the written word. It cannot be eaten or worn; it cannot cure disease; it cannot dissipate pollution, defang a racist, cause a spoonful of heroin to disintegrate. But, at the right time, in the right circumstances, falling on the right mind, a word may take effect. (Greenfield, 1975, p. 624)

Greenfield is too modest. Even in these days of interactive video and frenetic television programming, words on the printed page still have a powerful effect, as teachers well know. Imaginations and hearts soar when children are read to or read for themselves!

Children's Books and Recordings

Adler, D.A. (1989). *A picture book of Martin Luther King, Jr.* New York: Holiday House.

Adoff, A. (1973). *Black is brown is tan.* New York: Harper & Row.

Adoff, A. (1982). *All the colors of the race.* New York: Lothrop.

Aliki. (1976). *Corn is maise.* New York: Crowell.

Amon, A. (1981). *The earth is sore: Native Americans on nature.* New York: Atheneum.

Ancona, G. (1985). *Helping out.* New York: Clarion.

Andrews, J. (1986). *Very last first time.* New York: Atheneum.

Anno, M. (1986). *All in a day.* New York: Philomel.

Anzaldua, G. (1993). *Friends from the other side/ Amigos del otro lado.* Emeryville, CA: Children's Book Press.

Barton, B. (1981). *Building a house.* New York: Greenwillow.

Baylor, B. (1976). *And it is still that way: Legends told by Arizona Indian children.* New York: Scribner's.

Baylor, B. (1981). *A god on every mountain top: Stories of southwest Indian sacred mountains.* New York: Scribner's.

Beekman, D. (1982). *Forest, village, town, city.* New York: Harper & Row.

Blanco, A. (1992). *The desert mermaid.* San Francisco: Children's Book Press.

Botting, T. (Trans.). (1975). *The mitten.* Moscow: Malysh Publishers.

Brenner, B. (1984). *Wagon wheels.* New York: Harper.

Brett, J. (1989). *The mitten.* New York: Putnam's.

Brown, T. (1985). *Hello, amigos!* New York: Holt.

Cameron, A. (1986). *More stories Julian tells.* New York: Knopf.

Cohlene, T. (1990). *Quillworker: A Cheyenne legend.* Mahwah, NJ: Watermill Press.

Cohlene, T. (1990). *Turquoise boy: A Navajo legend.* Mahwah, NJ: Watermill Press.

Costabel, E.D. (1986). *The Pennsylvania Dutch: Craftsmen and farmers.* New York: Atheneum.

Craft, R. (1989). *The day of the rainbow.* New York: Viking.

D'Alelio, J. (1989). *I know that building!* Washington, DC: National Trust for Historic Preservation.

Dalgliesh, A. (1954). *The courage of Sarah Noble.* New York: Macmillan.

Daly, N. (1985). *Not so fast Songololo.* New York: Viking Penguin.

Dault, G.M. (1990). *Children in photography: 150 years.* Firefly, 150 Sparks Ave., Willowdale, Ontario M2H 2S4 Canada.

Delacre, L. (1989). *Arroz con leche: Popular songs and rhymes from Latin America.* New York: Scholastic.

Delton, J. (1980). *My mother lost her job today.* Niles, IL: Whitman.

Dragonwagon, C. (1990). *Home place.* New York: Macmillan.

Escudie, R. (1988). *Paul and Sebastian.* Brooklyn: Kane-Miller.

Fahs, S.L., & Cobb. A. (1980). *Old tales for a new day: Early answers to life's eternal questions.* Buffalo: Prometheus.

Feeney, S. (1985). *Hawaii is a rainbow.* Honolulu: University of Hawaii Press.

Flournoy, V. (1985). *The patchwork quilt.* New York: Dial.

Freedman, R. (1980). *Immigrant kids.* New York: Dutton.

Freedman, R. (1987). *Indian chiefs.* New York: Holiday House.

Friedman, I.R. (1984). *How my parents learned to eat.* Boston: Houghton Mifflin.

Gantschev, I. (1985). *Two islands.* Salzburg: Verlag Neugebauer Press.

Garaway, M.K. (1989). *Ashkii and his grandfather.* Tuscon: Treasure Chest.

Garza, C.L. (1990). *Family pictures.* Emeryville, CA: Children's Book Press.

Gibbons, G. (1990). *How a house is built.* New York: Holiday.

Girard, L.W. (1988). *We adopted you, Benjamin Koo.* Niles, IL: Whitman.

Goble, P. (1984). *Buffalo woman.* New York: Aladdin.

Goble, P. (1988). *Her seven brothers.* New York: Bradbury.

Goldstein, A. (1979). *My very own Jewish home.* Kar-Ben Copies, 6800 Tildenwood Ln., Rockville, MD 20852.

Greenfield, E. (1981). *Daydreamers.* New York: Dial.

Greenfield, E. (1989). *Africa dream.* New York: Harper & Row.

Hall, D. (1979). *Ox-cart man.* New York: Puffin.

Hamilton, V. (1993). *Many thousand gone: African Americans from slavery to freedom.* New York: Knopf.

Havill, J. (1986). *Jamaica's find.* Boston: Houghton Mifflin.

Hazen, B.S. (1983). *Tight times.* New York: Penguin.

Hewett, J. (1990). *Hector lives in the U.S. now: The story of a Mexican-American child*. New York: Lippincott.

Highwater, J. (1981). *Moonsong lullaby*. New York: Lothrop, Lee & Shepard.

Howard, E.F. (1991). *Aunt Flossie's hats (and crab cakes later)*. New York: Clarion.

Jin, S. (1991). *My first American friend*. Milwaukee: Raintree.

Kalman, B., & Belsey, W. (1988). *An Arctic community*. New York: Crabtree.

Kandoian, E. (1989). *Is anybody up?* New York: Putnam.

Kuklin, S. (1992). *How my family lives in America*. New York: Bradbury.

Lasky, K. (1980). *The weaver's gift*. New York: Warne.

Lessac, F. (1985). *My little island*. New York: Lippincott.

Lionni, L. (1968). *Swimmy*. New York: Pantheon.

Livingston, M.C. (Ed.). (1990). *Dog poems*. New York: Holiday House.

Loh, M. (1987). *Tucking mommy in*. New York: Orchard.

Martel, C. (1976). *Yagua days*. New York: Dial.

Mathieu, J. (1979). *The olden days*. New York: Random House.

Mattox, C.W. (Ed.). (1989). *Shake it to the one that you love the best: Play songs and lullabies from Black musical traditions*. Warren-Mattox, 3817 San Pablo Dam Rd., #336, El Sobrante, CA 94803. (Available on cassette from Music for Little People)

Maury, I. (1979). *My mother and I are growing strong/ Mi mama y yo nos hacemos fuertes*. Berkeley: New Seed Press.

McMillan, B. (1990). *One sun: A book of terse verse*. New York: Holiday House.

Meyer, L.D. (1988). *Harriet Tubman: They called me Moses*. Parenting Press, 7744 31st Ave., N.E., Seattle, WA 98115.

Morris, A. (1989). *Bread, bread, bread*. New York: Lothrop, Lee & Shepard.

Morris, A. (1990). *On the go*. New York: Lothrop, Lee & Shepard.

Music for Little People. (1989). *Peace is the world smiling* (CD Recording MLP D–2104). Redway, CA: Author.

National Geographic Society. (1989). *Exploring your world: The adventure of geography*. Washington, DC: Author.

New World Records. (1976). *Songs of earth, water, fire and sky: Music of the American Indian* (CD Recording No. 80246–2). New York: Author.

Oakley, R. (1989). *Games children play around the world*. (Series includes strength and skill, chanting.) New York: Marshall Cavendish.

Ortiz, S. (1988). *The people shall continue*. San Francisco: Children's Book Press.

Ovale, Inc. (1981). *Hiver*. (Also *Printemps, Eté, Automne*). Sillery, Québec, Canada: Author.

Pomerantz, C. (1989). *The chalk doll*. New York: Lippincott.

Provensen, A., & Provensen, M. (1987). *Shaker Lane*. New York: Viking Kestrel.

Rabe, B. (1981). *The balancing girl*. New York: Elsevier-Dutton.

Rogers, F. (1987). *Making friends*. New York: Putnam.

Roy, R. (1990). *Whose hat is that?* New York: Clarion.

Say, A. (1991). *Tree of cranes*. New York: Houghton Mifflin.

Schlank, C.H., & Metzger, B. (1990). *Martin Luther King, Jr.: A biography for young children*. Mt. Rainier, MD: Gryphon House.

Seuss, D. (1984). *The butter battle book*. New York: Random House.

Sewall, M. (1990). *People of the breaking day*. New York: Atheneum.

Shachtman, T. (1989). *The president builds a house*. New York: Simon & Schuster.

Showers, P. (1965). *Your skin and mine*. New York: Harper.

Simon, N. (1975). *All kinds of families*. Niles, IL: Whitman.

Slobodkina, E. (1948). *Caps for sale*. New York: Harper & Row.

Smith, K. (1990). *Cherokee legends I* (Cassette Recording). Cherokee, NC: Cherokee Publications.

Sneve, V.D.H. (1989). *Dancing teepees: Poems of American Indian youth*. New York: Holiday House.

Soya, K. (1986). *A house of leaves*. New York: Philomel.

Steptoe, J. (1987). *Mufaro's beautiful daughters*. New York: Lothrop, Lee & Shepard.

Stoltz, M. (1988). *Storm in the night*. New York: Harper.

Sweet Honey in the Rock. (1990). *All for freedom* (Cassette Recording). Redway, CA: Music for Little People.

Tran-Khan-Tuyet. (1986). *The little weaver of Thai-Yen village*. San Francisco: Children's Book Press.

Travers, P.L. (1980). *Two pairs of shoes*. New York: Viking.

Tresselt, A. (1964). *The mitten*. New York: Scholastic.

Uchida, Y. (1984). *A jar of dreams*. New York: Atheneum.

Weitzman, D. (1975). *My backyard history book*. Boston: Little, Brown.

Wilder, L.E. (1953). *Little house on the prairie*. New York: Harper & Row.

Wilder, L.E. (1953). *On the banks of Plum Creek*. New York: Harper & Row.

Xiong, B. (1989). *Nine-in-one Grr! Grr!* Emeryville, CA: Children's Book Press.

Yarbrough, C. (1979). *Cornrows*. New York: Putnam.

Yee, S., & Kokin, L. (1977). *Got me a story to tell: Five children tell about their lives*. St. John's Education Threshold, 1661 15th St., San Francisco, CA 94103.

Youldon, G. (1979). *Les nombres*. Montreal: Granger Freres Limité.

Resources for Teachers: Publishers, Organizations, and Suppliers of Educational Materials

Adoptive Families of America
3333 Highway 100 North
Minneapolis, MN 55422
612–535–4829

Adventures in Rhythm
1844 North Mohawk St.
Chicago, IL 60614
312–337–5014

Afro-Am Distributing Co.
819 S. Wabash Ave.
Suite 610
Chicago, IL 60605
312–791–1611

AIMS International Books, Inc.
7709 Hamilton Ave.
Cincinnati, OH 45231–3103
800–733–2067

Alcazar, Inc.
P.O. Box 429
Waterbury, VT 05676
800–541–9904

American Indians Series
Time-Life Books
1450 E. Parham Rd.
Richmond, VA 23280
800–621–7026

Americans All
6011 Blair Rd., N.W.
Washington, DC 20011
202–832–0330

Animal Town
P.O. Box 485
Healdsburg, CA 95448
800–445–8642

Anti-Defamation League
720 Market St.
Suite 800
San Francisco, CA 94102
415–981–3500

Arcoiris Records
P.O. Box 7428
Berkeley, CA 94707
510–527–5539

Arte Publico Press
University of Houston
MDA Library
Room 2
Houston, TX 77204–2090
713–743–2841

Association on American Indian Affairs
245 Fifth Ave.
Suite 1801
New York, NY 10016
212–689–8720

Association for Childhood Education International (ACEI)
11501 Georgia Ave.
Suite 315
Wheaton, MD 20902
301–942–2443

Association for the Study of Afro-American Life and History
1407 14th St., N.W.
Washington, DC 20005
202–667–2822

Bilingual Publications Co., The
270 Lafayette St.
New York, NY 10012
212–431–3500

Biracial Family Network
P.O. Box 489
Chicago, IL 60653-0489
312–288–3644

Bookmen, Inc., The
Dick Humphrey, librarian
525 North Third St.
Minneapolis, MN 55401
800–328–8411

California Tomorrow—Immigrant Students Project
Fort Mason Center
Building B
San Francisco, CA 94123
415–441–7631

Canyon Records & Indian Arts
4143 North 16th St.
Phoenix, AZ 85016
602–266–4823

Center for Teaching International Relations
University of Denver
Denver, CO 80208
303–871–2164

Center for the Improvement of Child Caring
Effective Black Parenting Program
11331 Ventura Blvd.
Suite 103
Studio City, CA 91604
818–980–0903

Center for the Study of Biracial Children
2300 South Krameria St.
Denver, CO 80222
303–692–9008

Cherokee Publications
P.O. Box 430
Cherokee, NC 28719
704–488–2988

Children's Book Council
568 Broadway
Suite 404
New York, NY 10012
212–966–1990

Children's Book Press
6400 Hollis St.
Suite 4
Emeryville, CA 94608
510–655–3395

Children's Creative Response to Conflict
Fellowship of Reconciliation
Box 271
523 North Broadway
Nyack, NY 10960
914–358–4601

Children's Defense Fund
25 E St., N.W.
Washington, DC 20001
202–628–8787

Children's Foundation, The
725 Fifteenth St., N.W.
Suite 505
Washington, DC 20005
202–347–3300

Children's Small Press Collection
719 North 4th Ave.
Ann Arbor, MI 48104
313–668–8056

Claudia's Caravan
P.O. Box 1582
Alameda, CA 94501
510–521–7871

Cobblestone Publishing, Inc.
7 School St.
Peterborough, NH 03458–1454
800–821–0115

Council for Early Childhood Professional Recognition
1341 G St., N.W.
Suite 400
Washington, DC 20005
202–265–9090

Council for Exceptional Children
1920 Association Dr.
Reston, VA 22091
703–620–3660

Culturally Relevant Anti-Bias Leadership Project
Pacific Oaks College
5 Westmoreland Pl.
Pasadena, CA 91103
818–397–1306

Denver Indian Center, Inc., The
4407 Morrison Rd.
Denver, CO 80219
303–936–2688

Desmond A. Reid Enterprises
33 Lafayette Ave.
Brooklyn, NY 11217
718–625–4651

Disability Rights Education and Defense Fund
1633 Q St., N.W.
Suite 220
Washington, DC 20009
202–986–0375

East Wind Books and Arts
1435A Stockton St.
San Francisco, CA 94133
415–772–5877

Educational Equity Concepts, Inc.
114 East 32nd St.
Suite 701
New York, NY 10016
212–725–1803

Educational Record Center
3233 Burnt Mill Dr.
Suite 100
Wilmington, NC 28403
800–438–1637

ERIC Clearinghouse on Elementary and Early Childhood Education
University of Illinois
805 West Pennsylvania Ave.
Urbana, IL 61801
217–333–1386

Four Winds
P.O. Box 544
York, NE 68467
800–775–3125

Fulcrum Publishing
350 Indiana St.
Suite 350
Golden, CO 80401
303–277–1623

Global Village, Inc.
2210 Wilshire Blvd.
Box 262
Santa Monica, CA 90403
213–459–5188
800–955–GLOBAL

Graywolf Press
2402 University Ave.
Suite 203
St. Paul, MN 55114
612–641–0077

Green Circle, Inc.
1300 Spruce St.
Philadelphia, PA 19107
215–893–8400

Gryphon House
P.O. Box 275
Mt. Rainier, MD 20712
800–638–0928

Hearts & Minds
234 East Main St.
Dallastown, PA 17313
717–246–3333

Heritage Key, Inc., The
6102 East Nescal
Scottsdale, AZ 85254
602–483–3313

Hispanic Book Distributors, Inc.
1665 West Grant Rd.
Tucson, AZ 85745
800–634–2124

Holistic Education Press
P.O. Box 328
Brandon, VT 05733–0328
802–247–8312

Human Policy Press
P.O. Box 127
Syracuse, NY 13210
315–443–3851

Iaconi Book Imports, Inc.
1110 Mariposa St.
San Francisco, CA 94107
800–955–9557

Institute for Peace and Justice
4144 Lindell Blvd.
Room 124
St. Louis, MO 63108
314–533–4445

Inter-Hemispheric Education Resource Center
Box 4506
Albuquerque, NM 87196
505–842–8288

Japanese American Curriculum Project
P.O. Box 1587
234 Main St.
San Mateo, CA 94401
415–343–9408

Jesana Ltd.
P.O. Box 17
Irvington, NY 10533–2317
800–443–4728

Lakeshore Learning Materials
2695 East Dominguez St.
P.O. Box 6261
Carson, CA 90749
800–421–5354

Lectorum Publications, Inc.
137 West 14th St.
New York, NY 10011
800–345–5946

LIFT EVERY VOICE Multicultural and Minority Source Materials Co.
16 Park Ln.
Newton Centre, MA 02159
617–244–9808

Lollipop Power Books
Carolina Wren Press
120 Morris St.
Durham, NC 27701
919–560–2738

Music for Little People
P.O. Box 1460
Redway, CA 95560
800–727–2233

National Association for Bilingual Education
1220 L St., N.W.
Suite 605
Washington, DC 20005–4018
202–898–1829

National Association for the Education of Young Children
1509 16th St., N.W.
Washington, DC 20036–1426
202–232–8777

National Black Child Development Institute
1023 15th St., N.W.
#600
Washington, DC 20005
202–387–1281

National Center for Research on Cultural Diversity and Second Language Learning
399 Clark Kerr Hall
University of California, Santa Cruz
Santa Cruz, CA 95064
408–459–3500

National Clearinghouse for Bilingual Education
George Washington University
1118 22nd St., N.W.
Washington, DC 20037
800–321–NCBE, 202–467–0867

National Coalition of Education Activists
P.O. Box 405
Rosendale, NY 12472
914–658–8115

National Council of La Raza
810 First St., N.E.
Suite 300
Washington, DC 20002
202–289–1380

National Gallery of Art
Publications Mail Order Dept.
2000 South Club Dr.
Landover, MD 20785
301–322–5900

National Institute Against Prejudice and Violence
University of Maryland
712 West Lombard St.
Baltimore, MD 21201
410–706–5170

National Museum of the American Indian
Smithsonian Institution
3753 Broadway at 155th St.
New York, NY 10032
212–283–2420

National PTA
700 North Rush St.
Chicago, IL 60611–2571
312–787–0977

Native American Authors Distribution Project
c/o The Greenfield Review Press
2 Middle Grove Rd.
P.O. Box 308
Greenfield Center, NY 12833
518–584–1728

Network of Educators on the Americas
1118 22nd St., N.W.
Washington, DC 20037
202–429–0137

New Society Publishers
4527 Springfield Ave.
Philadelphia, PA 19143
800–333–9093
P.O. Box 189
Gabriola Island
British Columbia
Canada V0R 1X0
604–247–9737

Northland Poster Collective
P.O. Box 7096
Minneapolis, MN 55407–1831
800–627–3082

PBS Video
1320 Braddock Pl.
Alexandria, VA 22314–1698
800–424–7963

Peace Works, Inc.
3812 North First St.
Fresno, CA 93726
800–445–8585

People of Every Stripe
P.O. Box 12505
Portland, OR 97212
503–224–8057

Phi Delta Kappa Education Foundation
P.O. Box 789
408 North Union St.
Bloomington, IN 47402–0789
812–339–1156

PlayFair Toys
P.O. Box 18210
Boulder, CO 80308
800–824–7255

Portfolio Project, Inc. The
6011 Blair Rd., N.W.
Washington, DC 20011
202–832–0330

Pueblo to People
2105 Silber Rd.
Suite 101
Houston, TX 77055–2545
713–956–1172, 800–843–5257

Raintree Publishers
310 West Wisconsin Ave.
Milwaukee, WI 53203
800–558–7264

Red and Black Books
432 15th Ave. East
Seattle, WA 98112
206–322–7323

Redleaf Press
450 North Syndicate
Suite 5
St. Paul, MN 55104–4125
800–423–8309

Rethinking Schools
1001 East Keefe Ave.
Milwaukee, WI 53212–1710
414–964–9646

Rounder Records
One Camp St.
Cambridge, MA 02140
617–354–0700

Savanna Books
858 Massachusetts Ave.
Cambridge, MA 02139
617–868–3423

Smithsonian Institution Press
Dept. 900
Blue Ridge Summit, PA 17294–
0900
800–782–4612

Southern Early Childhood Association
P.O. Box 56130
Brady Station
Little Rock, AR 72215
501–663–0353

Spanish Books, Inc.
6364 El Cajon Blvd.
Suite A
San Diego, CA 92115
619–229–0188

Syracuse Cultural Workers
P.O. Box 6367
Syracuse, NY 13217
315–474–1132

Thomas Moore Records
5532 Providence Rd.
Charlotte, NC 28226
704–529–4725

United Indians of All Tribes Foundation
Daybreak Star Indian Cultural Center
Box 99100
Seattle, WA 98199
206–285–4425

Weston Woods
Weston, CT 06883–1199
800–243–5020

Winston-Dereck Publishers, Inc.
P.O. Box 90883
Nashville, TN 37209
615–329–1319

Women's Action Alliance
370 Lexington Ave.
#603
New York, NY 10017
212–532–8330

Bibliography

Abramson, S., Seda, I., & Johnson, C. (1990). Literacy development in a multilingual kindergarten classroom. *Childhood Education, 67*(2), 68–72.

Allen, J., Freeman, P., & Osborne, S. (1989). Research in review. Children's political knowledge and attitudes. *Young Children, 44*(2), 57–61.

Alter, J., & Denworth, L. (1990). A (vague) sense of history: Ignorance of history affects our future as a democratic nation and as individuals. *Newsweek Special Edition: Education: A Consumer's Handbook,* pp. 31–33.

American Demographics. (1991). *American diversity: What the 1990 Census reveals about population growth, blacks, Hispanics, Asians, ethnic diversity, and children—and what it means to you.* Ithaca, NY: Author.

Aptheker, H. (Ed.). (1990). *A documentary history of the Negro people of the United States* (Vols. 1–4). New York: Citadel.

Archer, K. (1990, June 20). Black parents still fighting slavery. *Tulsa World,* p. A1.

Association for Supervision and Curriculum Development. (1991). The quest for higher standards. *Educational Leadership, 48*(5), 1–104.

Bach, R. (1977). *Illusions: The adventures of a reluctant messiah.* New York: Laurel.

Bailey, T.A. (1966). *The American pageant. Vol. 1* (3rd ed.). Boston: Heath.

Berger, E.H. (1991). *Parents as partners in education: The school and home working together* (3rd ed.). Columbus, OH: Macmillan.

Bigelow, B., Miner, B., & Peterson, B. (Eds.). (1991). *Rethinking Columbus.* Milwaukee: Rethinking Schools.

Billman, J. (1992). The Native American curriculum: Attempting alternatives to tepees and headbands. *Young Children, 47*(6), 22–25.

Bjorklund, G., & Burger, C. (1987). Making conferences work for parents, teachers, and children. *Young Children, 42*(2), 26–31.

Boutte, G.S., & McCromick, C.B. (1992). Authentic multicultural activities: Avoiding pseudomulticulturalism. *Childhood Education, 68*(3), 140–144.

Brady, P. (1992). Columbus and the quincentennial myths: Another side of the story. *Young Children, 47*(6), 4–14.

Branden, N. (1985). *Honoring the self: The psychology of confidence and respect.* New York: Bantam.

Bredekamp, S. (Ed.). (1987). *Developmentally appropriate practice in early childhood programs serving children from birth through age 8* (exp. ed.). Washington, DC: NAEYC.

Bruchac, J. (1991). *Keepers of the earth: Native American stories* (Audiotape). Golden, CO: Fulcrum.

Byrnes, D.A., & Kiger, G. (1992). *Common bonds: Anti-bias teaching in a diverse society.* Wheaton, MD: Association for Childhood Education International.

Caduto, M.J., & Bruchac, J. (1988). *Keepers of the earth. Teacher's guide. Native American stories and environmental activities for children.* Golden, CO: Fulcrum.

Caduto, M.J., & Bruchac, J. (1989). *Keepers of the earth: Native American stories and environmental activities for children.* Golden, CO: Fulcrum.

Cannella, G.S. (1986). Research: Praise and concrete rewards: Concerns for childhood education. *Childhood Education, 62*(4), 297–301.

Carlsson-Paige, N., & Levin, D.E. (1986). *The butter battle book*: Uses and abuses with young children. *Young Children, 41*(3), 37–42.

Carlsson-Paige, N., & Levin, D.E. (1992). Making peace in violent times: A constructivist approach to conflict resolution. *Young Children, 48*(1), 4–13.

Christopher, G.C. (1990). *The peopling of America: A teacher's manual for the Americans All program.* Washington, DC: The Portfolio Project.

Clark, L., DeWolf, S., & Clark, C. (1992). Teaching teachers to avoid having culturally assaultive classrooms. *Young Children, 47*(5), 4–9.

Clay, J.W. (1990). Working with lesbian and gay parents and their children. *Young Children, 45*(3), 31–35.

Clemens, S.G. (1988). A Dr. Martin Luther King, Jr. curriculum: Playing the dream. *Young Children, 43*(2), 6–11, 59–63.

Clements, D.H., Nastasi, B.K., & Swaminathan, S. (1993). Research in review. Young children and computers: Crossroads and directions from research. *Young Children, 48*(2), 56–64.

Comer, J.P. (1988a). Educating poor minority children. *Scientific American, 259*(5), 42–48.

Comer, J.P. (1988b). Teaching social skills to at-risk children. *Education Week, VII*(13), 28.

Coopersmith, S. (1967). *The antecedents of self-esteem.* Los Angeles: Freeman.

Copage, E.V. (1991). *Kwanzaa: An African-American celebration of culture and cooking.* New York: Morrow.

Corbett, S. (1993). A complicated bias. *Young Children, 48*(3), 29–31.

Council on Interracial Books for Children (CIBC). (n.d.). *Ten quick ways to analyze children's books for racism and sexism.* New York: Author.

Crary, E. (1984). *Kids can cooperate: A practical guide to teaching problem solving.* New York: Parenting Press.

Curry, N.E., & Johnson, C.N. (1990). *Beyond self-esteem: Developing a genuine sense of human value.* Washington, DC: NAEYC.

Derman-Sparks, L. (1989, Fall). How well are we nurturing racial and ethnic diversity? *CAEYC Connections,* pp. 3–5.

Derman-Sparks, L. (1992). "It isn't fair!" Antibias curriculum for young children. In B. Neugebauer (Ed.), *Alike and different: Exploring our humanity with young children* (rev. ed.) (pp. 2–10). Washington, DC: NAEYC.

Derman-Sparks, L., & the A.B.C. Task Force. (1989). *Anti-bias curriculum: Tools for empowering young children.* Washington, DC: NAEYC. (Also available as a videotape, *Anti-Bias Curriculum,* elaborating on these ideas. Order from Pacific Oaks College Bookstore, 5 Westmoreland Pl., Pasadena, CA 91103.)

Derman-Sparks, L., Gutiérriez, M., & Phillips, C.B. (1989). *Teaching young children to resist bias: What parents can do* (brochure). Washington, DC: NAEYC.

Feeney, S., & Moravcik, E. (1987). A thing of beauty: Aesthetic development in young children. *Young Children, 42*(6), 6–15.

First, J., & Carrera, J. (1988). *New voices: Immigrant students in U.S. public schools.* Boston: The National Coalition of Advocates for Students.

Fischer, K.W., & Bullock, D. (1984). Cognitive development in school-age children: Conclusions and new directions. In W.A. Collins (Ed.), *Development during middle childhood: The years from six to twelve* (pp. 70–146). Washington, DC: National Academy Press.

Foerster, L.M., & Little Soldier, D. (1978). Learning centers for young Native Americans. *Young Children, 33*(3), 53–57.

Fromboluti, C.S. (1990). *Helping your child learn geography.* Pueblo, CO: Consumer Information Center.

Froschl, M., Colon, L., Rubin, E., & Sprung, B. (1984). *Including all of us: An early childhood curriculum about disability.* New York: Educational Equity Concepts.

Fry-Miller, K., & Myers-Wall, J. (1988). *Young peacemakers project book.* Elgin, IL: Brethren Press.

Gardner, H. (1991). The school of the future. In J. Brockman (Ed.), *Ways of knowing: Reality Club III* (pp. 199–217). New York: Prentice-Hall.

Gareau, M., & Kennedy, C. (1991). Structure time and space to promote pursuit of learning in the primary grades. *Young Children, 46*(4), 46–50.

Gartrell, D. (1987). Assertive discipline: Unhealthy for children and other living things. *Young Children, 42*(2), 10–11.

Glover, M.K. (1990). A bag of hair: American 1st-graders experience Japan. *Childhood Education, 66*(3), 155–159.

Gottfried, A.E. (1983). Research in review. Intrinsic motivation in young children. *Young Children, 39*(1), 64–73.

Grammar, R. (1986). *Teaching peace* (cassette recording). Toronto: Children's Group, Inc. (Distributed in the United States by Alcazar Inc.)

Greenberg, P. (1988). Ideas that work with young children. The difficult child. *Young Children, 43*(5), 60–68.

Greenberg, P. (1989). Parents as partners in young children's development and education: A new American fad? Why does it matter? *Young Children, 44*(4), 61–75.

Greenberg, P. (1992a). Ideas that work with young children. How to institute some simple democratic practices pertaining to respect, rights, roots, and responsibilities in any classroom (without losing your leadership position). *Young Children, 47*(5), 10–17.

Greenberg, P. (1992b). Teaching about Native Americans? Or teaching about people, including Native Americans? *Young Children, 47*(6), 27–30, 79–81.

Greenfield, E. (1975). Something to shout about. *The Horn Book Magazine, 51*(6), 624–626.

Hale, J. (1991). The transmission of cultural values to young African American children. *Young Children, 46*(6), 7–15.

Harris, V.J. (1991). Research in review. Multicultural curriculum: African American children's literature. *Young Children, 46*(2), 37–44.

Hatcher, B., Pape, D., & Nicosia, R.T. (1988). Group games for global awareness. *Childhood Education, 65*(1), 8–13.

Haugland, S.W., & Shade, D.D. (1988). Developmentally appropriate software for young children. *Young Children, 43*(4), 37–43.

Head Start Bureau. (1992). *Multicultural principles for Head Start programs.* Washington, DC: Author.

Hearst, M.R. (Ed.). (1993). *Interracial identity: Celebration, conflict or choice?* Chicago: Biracial Family Network.

Hendrick, J. (1992). Where does it all begin? Teaching the principles of democracy in the early years. *Young Children, 47*(3), 51–53.

Herrera, J.F., & Wooden, S.L. (1988). Some thoughts about effective parent-school communication. *Young Children, 43*(6), 78–80.

Hilliard, A.G., III. (1989, January). Teachers and cultural styles in a pluralistic society. *NEA Today*, pp. 65–69.

Hirsch, E.S. (Ed.). (1984). *The block book* (rev. ed). Washington, DC: NAEYC.

Hitz, R., & Driscoll, A. (1988). Praise or encouragement? New insights into praise: Implications for early childhood teachers. *Young Children, 43*(5), 6–13.

Holt, B-G. (1989). *Science with young children* (rev. ed.). Washington, DC: NAEYC.

Honig, A.S. (1987). *Love & learn: Discipline for young children* (brochure). Washington, DC: NAEYC.

Hopkins, S., & Winters, J. (1990). *Discover the world: Empowering children to value themselves, others and the earth.* Santa Cruz, CA: New Society Publishers.

Jefferson, B. (1963). *The color book craze.* Wheaton, MD: Association for Childhood Education International.

Jones, M., Jr. (1991, September 9). It's a not so small world: Multiculturalism is broadening the horizons of children's literature. *Newsweek*, pp. 64–65.

Kamii, C., & DeVries, R. (1980). *Group games in early education: Implications of Piaget's theory.* Washington, DC: NAEYC.

Katz, L.G., & Chard, S.C. (1989). *Engaging children's minds: The project approach.* Norwood, NJ: Ablex.

Kendall, F.E. (1983). *Diversity in the classroom: A multicultural approach to the education of young children.* New York: Teachers College Press.

Kendall, F.E. (1988, November/December). Creating a multicultural environment. *Scholastic Today*, pp. 39–51.

Koeppel, J., with Mulrooney, M. (1992). The Sister Schools Program: A way for children to learn about cultural diversity—When there isn't any in their school. *Young Children, 48*(1), 44–47.

Kohn, A. (1991). Group grade grubbing versus cooperative learning. *Educational Leadership, 48*(5), 83–87.

Lally, J.R., Mangione, P.L., Honig, A.S., & Wittmer, D.S. (1988). More pride, less delinquency: Findings from the ten-year follow-up study of the Syracuse University Family Development Research Program. *Zero to 3, 8*(4), 13–18.

Lane, M. (1984). Reaffirmations: Speaking out for children. A child's right to the valuing of diversity. *Young Children, 39*(6), 76.

Lazar, I., & Darlington, R. (1982). *Lasting effects of early education: A report from the Consortium for Longitudinal Studies.* Monographs of the Society for Research in Child Development, 47(3, Serial No. 195).

Lee, E. (1992). The crisis in education: Forging an anti-racist response. *Rethinking Schools, 7*(1), 4–5.

Leslie, C. (1991, February 11). Classrooms of Babel: A record number of immigrant children pose[s] new problems for schools. *Newsweek*, pp. 56–57.

Little Soldier, L.M. (1989). Children as cultural anthropologists. *Childhood Education, 66*(2), 88–91.

Little Soldier, L.M. (1992). Building optimum learning environments for Navajo students. *Childhood Education, 68*(3), 145–148.

Little Soldier, L. (1992). Working with Native American children. *Young Children, 47*(6), 15–21.

Lynch, E.W., & Hanson, M.J. (1992). *Developing cross-cultural competence: A guide for working with young children and their families.* Baltimore: Paul H. Brookes.

Manley, R. (n.d.). *The vanishing Indian. Ray Manley: A portfolio.* Tuscon: Ray Manley Publishing. (English, German, and Japanese captions)

Maslow, A.H. (1954). *Motivation and personality.* New York: Harper & Row.

Maynard, F. (1989, September). Can you praise a child too much? *Parents*, pp. 93–96.

McCracken, J.B. (Ed.). (1990). *Helping children love themselves and others: A professional handbook for family day care.* Washington, DC: Children's Foundation.

McCracken, J.B. (1992). *Teacher's guide to learning activities: Grades K–2.* Washington, DC: Americans All.

McCracken, J.B. (Ed.). (In press). *Everyone counts: Applying Head Start's multicultural principles in all program components.* Washington, DC: Head Start Bureau.

Meddin, B.J., & Rosen, A.L. (1986). Child abuse and neglect: Prevention and reporting. *Young Children, 41*(4), 26–30.

Miller, C.S. (1984). Building self-control: Discipline for young children. *Young Children, 40*(1), 15–19.

Miner, B. (1992–93). Why students should study history: An interview with Howard Zinn. *Rethinking Schools, 7*(2), 6–8.

Morris, L. (Ed.). (1986). *Extracting learning styles from social/cultural diversity: A study of five American minorities.* Washington, DC: U.S. Office of Education, Southwest Teacher Corps Network.

Morrow, R.D. (1989). What's in a name? In particular, a Southeast Asian name? *Young Children, 44*(6), 20–23.

Myers, B.K., & Martin, M.P. (1993). Faith foundations for all of our children. *Young Children, 48*(2), 49–55.

National Association for the Education of Young Children (NAEYC). (1986). *Helping children learn self-control: A guide to discipline* (brochure). Washington, DC: Author.

National Association for the Education of Young Children & National Association of Early Childhood Specialists in State Departments of Education (NAEYC & NAECS/SDE). (1991). Guidelines for appropriate curriculum content and assessment in programs serving children ages three through eight. *Young Children, 46*(3), 21–38.

National Association of Elementary School Principals (NAESP). (1990). *Early childhood education and the elementary school principal: Standards for quality programs for young children.* Alexandria, VA: Author.

National Association of State Boards of Education (NASBE). (1988). *Right from the start. The report of the NASBE Task Force on Early Childhood Education.* Alexandria, VA: Author.

National Association of State Boards of Education (NASBE). (1991). *Caring communities: Supporting young children and families. The report of the National Task Force on School Readiness.* Alexandria, VA: Author.

National Parent-Teacher Association & Anti-Defamation League of B'nai B'rith. (1989). *What to tell your child about prejudice and discrimination.* Chicago: Author.

Nelsen, J. (1987). *Positive discipline.* New York: Ballantine.

Neugebauer, B. (1990). Going one step further—No traditional holidays. *Child Care Information Exchange,* (74), 42.

Neugebauer, B. (Ed.). (1992). *Alike and different: Exploring our humanity with young children* (rev. ed.). Washington, DC: NAEYC.

Ogbu, J.U. (1987). Opportunity structure, cultural boundaries, and literacy. In J.A. Langer (Ed.), *Language, literacy, and culture: Issues of society and schooling* (pp. 149–177). Norwood, NJ: Ablex.

Orlick, T. (1978). *The cooperative sports and games book: Challenge without competition.* New York: Pantheon.

Oyemade, U.J., & Washington, V. (1989). Drug abuse prevention begins in early childhood (and is much more than a matter of instructing young children about drugs!). *Young Children, 44*(5), 6–12.

Pechman, E.M. (1992). Child as meaning maker: The organizing theme for professional practice schools. In M. Levine (Ed.), *Professional practice schools: Reflections of school reform in teacher education.* New York: Teachers College Press.

Pederson, P. (1988). *A handbook for developing multicultural awareness.* Alexandria, VA: American Association for Counseling and Development.

Perry, T., & Fraser, J.W. (1993). Reconstructing schools as multicultural democracies. *Rethinking Schools, 7*(3), 16–17, 31.

Phillips, C.B. (1988). Nurturing diversity for today's children and tomorrow's leaders. *Young Children, 43*(2), 42–47.

Ramsey, P.G. (1979). Beyond "Ten Little Indians" and turkeys: Alternative approaches to Thanksgiving. *Young Children, 34*(6), 28–32, 49–52.

Ramsey, P.G. (1982). Multicultural education in early childhood. *Young Children, 37*(2), 13–24.

Ramsey, P.G., Vold, E.B., & Williams, L.R. (1989). *Multicultural education: A source book.* New York: Garland.

Richards, B. (1976). Mapping: An introduction to symbols. *Young Children, 31*(2), 145–156.

Rigg, P., Kazemek, F.E., & Hudelson, S. (1993). Children's books about the elderly. *Rethinking Schools, 7*(3), 25.

Rogers, C. (1961). *On becoming a person.* Boston: Houghton Mifflin.

Root, M.P.P. (Ed.). (1992). *Racially mixed people in America.* Newbury Park, CA: Sage.

Sale, K. (1990). *The conquest of paradise: Christopher Columbus and the Columbian legacy.* New York: Penguin.

Schiller, P., & Bermudez, A.B. (1988). Working with non-English speaking children. *Texas Child Care Quarterly, 12*(3), 3–8.

Schmuck, R.A., & Schmuck, P.A. (1988). *Group processes in the classroom* (4th ed.). Dubuque, IA: Wm. C. Brown.

Schon, I. (1991). Recent noteworthy books in Spanish for young children. *Young Children, 46*(4), 65.

Schuman, J.M. (1981). *Art from many hands: Multicultural art projects.* Worcester, MA: Davis Publications.

Seefeldt, C. (1975). "Is today tomorrow?" History for young children. *Young Children, 30*(2), 99–105.

Seefeldt, C. (1984). What's in a name? Lots to learn! *Young Children, 39*(5), 24–30.

Seefeldt, C. (1993). Social studies: Learning for freedom. *Young Children, 48*(3), 4–9.

Seligmann, J. (1990). Speaking in tongues: Dios mio! Even Americans will need to know a foreign language to get along in the 21st century. *Newsweek Special Edition: Education: A Consumer's Handbook,* pp. 36–37.

Selye, H. (1976). *The stress of life* (rev. ed.). New York: McGraw-Hill.

Shure, M.B., & Spivack, G. (1978). *Problem-solving techniques in childrearing.* San Francisco: Jossey-Bass.

Simonson, R., & Walker, S. (Eds.). (1988). *Graywolf Annual Five: Multi-cultural literacy: Opening the American mind.* St. Paul, MN: Graywolf Press.

Skeen, P., Robinson, B.E., & Flake-Hobson, C. (1984). Blended families: Overcoming the Cinderella myth. *Young Children 40*(2), 64–74.

Slapin, B. (1990). *A guide to evaluating children's literature for handicappism.* Berkeley: Oyate.

Slapin, B., & Seale, D. (Eds.). (1992). *Through Indian eyes: The Native experience in books for children.* Philadelphia: New Society.

Slavin, R.E. (1991). Synthesis of research on co-operative learning. *Educational Leadership, 48*(5), 71–82.

Smith, C.A., & Davis, D.E. (1976). Teaching children non-sense. *Young Children, 31*(6), 438–447.

Smith, F. (1986). *Insult to intelligence: The bureaucratic invasion of our classrooms.* Portsmouth, NH: Heinemann.

Sobel, J. (1983). *Everybody wins: 393 non-competitive games for young children.* New York: Walker.

Soto, L.D. (1991). Research in review. Understanding bilingual/bicultural young children. *Young Children, 46*(2), 30–36.

Southern Early Childhood Association. (1989). *Multicultural education: A position statement.* Little Rock, AR: Author.

Spann, M.B. (1992). *Literature-based multicultural activities: An integrated approach.* New York: Scholastic.

Spottswood, R.K. (1989). *Music of America's peoples: A historical perspective.* Washington, DC: The Portfolio Project.

Steele, S. (1990). *The content of our character: A new vision of race in America.* New York: St. Martin's.

Stone, J.G. (1978). *A guide to discipline.* Washington, DC: NAEYC.

Thibault, J.P., & McKee, J.S. (1982). Practical parenting with Piaget. *Young Children, 38*(1), 18–27.

Trimble, S. (Ed.). (1986). *Our voices, our land.* Flagstaff, AZ: Northland.

Wardle, F. (1990a). Endorsing children's differences: Meeting the needs of adopted minority children. *Young Children, 45*(5), 44–46.

Wardle, F. (1990b). Bunny ears and cupcakes for all—Are parties developmentally appropriate? *Child Care Information Exchange,* (74), 39–41.

Wardle, F. (1992a). Building positive images: Interracial children and their families. In B. Neugebauer (Ed.), *Alike and different: Exploring our humanity with young children* (rev. ed.) (pp. 98–107). Washington, DC: NAEYC.

Wardle, F. (1992b). Supporting biracial children in the school setting. *Education and Treatment of Children, 15*(2), 163–172.

Weikart, D.P. (1989). *Quality preschool programs: A long-term social investment.* New York: Ford Foundation.

Weitzman, D. (1975). *My backyard history book.* Boston: Little, Brown.

West, B. (1992). Children are caught—between home and school, culture and school. In B. Neugebauer (Ed.), *Alike and different: Exploring our humanity with young children* (rev. ed.) (pp. 127–139). Washington, DC: NAEYC.

White, S.H., & Siegel, A.W. (1984). Cognitive development in time and space. In B. Rogoff & J. Lave (Eds.), *Everyday cognition: Its development in social context* (pp. 238–277). Cambridge, MA: Harvard University Press.

Wickens, E. (1993). Penny's question: "I will have a child in my class with two moms—What do you know about this?" *Young Children, 48*(3), 25–28.

Williams, L.R. (1989). Issues in education: Diverse gifts, multicultural education in the kindergarten. *Childhood Education, 66*(1), 2–3.

Williams, L.R., & De Gaetano, Y. (1985). *ALERTA: A multicultural, bilingual approach to teaching young children.* Menlo Park, CA: Addison-Wesley.

Wolfman, I. (1991). *Do people grow on family trees? Genealogy for kids and other beginners.* New York: Workman.

Women's International League for Peace and Freedom. (1989). Undoing racism. *Peace and Freedom, 49*(4), 5.

Wong Fillmore, L. (1990). Now or later? Issues related to the early education of minority group children. In *Early childhood and family education: Analysis and recommendations of the Council of Chief State School Officers.* New York: Harcourt Brace Jovanovich.

Wong Fillmore, L. (1991a). Language and cultural issues in the early education of language minority children. In S.L. Kagan (Ed.), *The care and education of America's young children: Obstacles and opportunities. 90th yearbook, Pt. 1,* (pp. 30–49). Chicago: National Society for the Study of Education.

Wong Fillmore, L. (1991b). Second language learning in children: A model of language learning in social context. In E. Bialystok (Ed.), *Language processing by bilingual children* (pp. 49–69). New York: Cambridge University Press.

Workman, S., & Anziano, M.C. (1993). Curriculum webs: Weaving connections from children to teachers. *Young Children, 48*(2), 4–9.

York, S. (1991). *Roots and wings: Affirming culture in early childhood programs.* St. Paul, MN: Redleaf Press.

Zinn, H. (1980). *A people's history of the United States.* New York: Harper & Row.

Index

Nelsen, J., 26, 52, 56–58, 59
Neugebauer, B., 29, 33, 61, 85, 86
New World Records, 81
Nicosia, R.T., 34, 87

Ogbu, J.U., 7
Orlick, T., 34
Oyemade, U.J., 66

Pape, D., 34, 87
Pechman, E.M., 11, 12
Perry, T., 10
Peterson, B., 85
Phillips, C.B., 7, 11, 12, 21, 32, 50
play, 39
praise, 52
prejudice, viii, 87
pride, 25, 26, 51, 52, 53, 54, 55–56
Puerto Ricans, 23, 79
punishment
        as artifical consequence, 58

races and cultures, viii
racism
        discrimination and stereotypes, 7
        institutional, 12
        patterns of and oppression, 8
        process of identifying, 8
        schools alone not making up for, 12
Ramsey, P.G., 22, 43, 85
reading, 19, 31, 33, 34, 86–87
        See also **literature, children's**
respect
        classrooms embedding, 6, 47, 48
        embedded in children, 4
        reflected in materials, 30
        universal concept of, viii
Richards, B., 37
rights
        basic—children's, vii
        civil, v, 19, 67
        human, v, 12
Robinson, B.E., 66
Root, M.P.P., 19
Rosen, A.L., 66
Roy, R., 68

Schiller, P., 53
Schuman, J.M., 44, 81
science, 48, 60, 61, 62, 65, 85
Seale, D., 85
Seda, I., 24, 84
Seefeldt, C., 16, 60, 84
self-esteem, 3
        See also **pride**
Shade, D.D., 31
Shure, M.B., 56, 58

Siegel, A.W., 11
similarities
        and commonalities, 10, 49, 72
        of all peoples, vii
Skeen, P., 66
Slapin, B., 85
Slavin, R.E., 26, 62
Slobodkina, E., 68
Smith, C.A., 56
Smith, F., 2, 3, 29
Sobel, J., 36
Soto, L.D., 53, 54
Spivack, G., 56, 58
Spottswood, R.K., 43
Stone, J.G., 56
storytellers, 19
success of children, 17, 55
        See also **children**
Swaminathan, S., 31
Sweet Honey in the Rock, 81

teaching
        America's children, 2
        approach, balanced/respectful/integrated,
        25
        professional practice, 49, 55
        strategies, 2, 30, 48, 49, 50, 52
        that encourages children, 53
        using open-ended questions, 75
traditions, 84
translating, 24
Tresselt, A., 33

values
        American, 10

Wardle, F., 52, 61, 66, 85
Washington, V., 66
webs
        clothing, 69
        experiencing Japan, 18
        food, 45
Weikart, D.P., 11
Weitzman, D., 14, 84
West, B., 67
White, S.H., 11
Wickens, E., 66
Wilder, L.E., 19
Williams, L.R., 53, 84
Wittmer, D.S., 11
Wolfman, I., 14, 84
Wong Fillmore, L., 53
Wooden, S.L., 66
Workman, S., 18
writing, children's, 31–32, 80, 84–85, 86

Zinn, H., 73